Ione Gamble is a writer and editor based in London. Founding *Polyester* zine at twenty years old, the publication has gone on to become one of the world's leading voices in intersectional feminist publishing. Focusing on the rise of social media and identity politics, Ione and *Polyester* have built a community of strong minded, marginalised people determined to carve their place in a world that continues to ignore them. She has been named an editor shaping the future of magazines by *i-D* magazine, and a New Debutante by *Tatler*. She is also the host of the *Polyester Podcast*. *Poor Little Sick Girls* is her debut book.

'A clear-sighted, critically needed skewering of hustle culture, wellness and modern feminism's blind spots, Ione pulls no punches in *Poor Little Sick Girls*. Everyone – and I mean everyone – should read this book.'
Yomi Adegoke

'A sizzling insight into how tropes about sick women and unacceptable bodies have been constructed throughout history through a cultural and personal lens. Ione writes with warmth, honesty and nuance, inviting the reader into a conversation that has, up until now, been afforded little space for exploration.'
Liv Little

'This book is smart, addictive, wry and insightful. At a time when online discourse feels so muddled, Ione manages to pick through the weeds with characteristic humour and nuance. This is the anti-girlboss Bible and I love it.'
Daisy Jones

'A thrilling exploration of the relationships between bodies, abstract forces like language and stereotypes, and the material conditions that shape young adults' lives.'
Tavi Gevinson

'Where so much online is generic and conformist, Ione Gamble's aesthetic and vision is anything but. A style icon and writer who seamlessly blends the esoteric and the obscure with popular culture as well as a commitment to many forms of social justice.'
Emma Dabiri

'One of the sharpest, wittiest and most incisive thinkers of her generation. I always want to hear Ione's perspective on feminism, culture, and art – or just about anything.'
Sirin Kale

'Incredible insight with a transgressive, witty, spirit.'
Courtney Love

'Ione's debut is a breath of fresh air. Both in the way she tackles the topic of feminism, and in the style its written. I want so many people to read this!'
Travis Alabanza

'Complicated and honest, bold and tender – *Poor Little Sick Girls* interrogates the problems people like to pretend aren't there. Essential reading.'
Annie Lord

'Gamble's essay collection promises to dispel wellness myths and the falsehoods of liberal feminism through her experiences of becoming ill in early adulthood, spending her 20th year in and out of doctors' rooms ... I languished in bed with my own copy, dog-earing every other page for its relatability and important reminders.'
Refinery29

'A crystal-clear mirror held up to contemporary feminism ... Ione Gamble examines feminism's fourth wave and its intersections with the internet and capitalism, to brilliant effect.'
i News

Poor Little Sick Girls

Ione Gamble

dialogue
books

DIALOGUE BOOKS

First published in Great Britain in 2022 by Dialogue
This paperback edition published in 2023 by Dialogue Books

1 3 5 7 9 10 8 6 4 2

A CIP catalogue record for this book is available from the British Library.

ISBN 978-0-349-70242-1

Typeset in Berling by M Rules
Printed and bound in Great Britain by Clays Ltd, Elcograf, S.p.A.

Papers used by Dialogue are from well-managed forests and other
responsible sources.

Dialogue Books
Carmelite House
50 Victoria Embankment
London EC4Y 0DZ

www.dialoguebooks.co.uk

Dialogue Books, part of Little Brown, Book Group Limited,
an Hachette UK company.

For Alfie. I love you.

Contents

Introduction

My body exists as a muddling mess
of illness and unanswered questions.
I've seen printed-out pictures of my
own insides taken with cameras inserted
down my throat, but I'm yet to be
convinced there is little more behind my
bones than a big black hole.

I've always had a complicated relationship with the void.

Defined by Oxford languages as: *noun: a completely empty space, 'the black void of space'.*

A vast emptiness, a concept to describe the incomprehensible. The void has become a catch-all among my generation for the general lack of purpose or feeling of belonging many experience when moving through the universe. Don't get me wrong, it's not as if I've never considered my place in the world, who I am and why I was put on the planet. I've read about existentialism; not from philosophers, but from women my age on the internet. I've scrolled through relatable viral tweet after relatable viral tweet about the vast emptiness of existence. I've even double-tapped a few. But on the whole, as someone who was diagnosed with a chronic illness in their late teens, the void itself has never been something I've fully understood or felt.

Growing up in the early age of social media, I was surrounded by my peers, wondering where they fitted in. First through the lens of teen angst and coming-of-age girl rage, filtered through confessional Tumblr posts and autobiographical artwork dealing with the trials and tribulations of growing up. I gazed at my laptop screen as accounts I followed banded together to take on the world's wrongs, to make sense of the mess that is femininity, and to push against the still restrictive stereotypes projected onto girls both on and off the internet. I admired those around me filling their voids with a sense of community, belonging and purpose. I gorged on the work published by people much more confident than me, unable to fully comprehend their confusion about our reality, but awe-struck by their ability to post their thoughts without fear of judgement.

My generation's struggle to get a grasp on what our place is doesn't subside as we enter adulthood. We're the least likely to own our own house, to marry, or to put down any tangible roots. We've had to grow up under right-wing governments who stripped away one by one the benefits experienced by our parents. However, while those around me bathe in uncertainty, I've always felt annoyingly sure of who I was meant to be. As a child, I would create mental checklists of what my adulthood would look like. I'd carve myself out full careers, choose which university course to study years before I could apply, and work quietly but tire-lessly to make sure my future would be the one I expected. Daydreaming about my future self was a far more effective form of escapism than any book, film or other outlet would allow me. I'd plan years of my life well in advance: where I would live, the type of work I would undertake. I spent my teen years convinced that my life would really start if I could just plan my future well enough to make it past growing up.

What I didn't account for in an infancy spent preparing for adulthood was being diagnosed with an incurable illness before I'd even turned twenty. Four months into my first year at university, I was rushed into the acute medical ward of Epsom Hospital following over six months of internal bleeding, weight loss, and a strange habit of fainting at any given moment. After spending the first twenty-four hours in a haze of sedation and confusion, I came to hooked up to a drip of steroids and being spoken to by doctors who provided few answers.

Even when faced with a world-altering medical condition, I remained irritatingly insistent that a diagnosis of Crohn's disease wouldn't screw up my plans. During my first hospital stay, I ignored the advice of doctors who urged me to rest, and instead made the astute decision to temporarily discharge myself to attend a seminar at university – despite medical professionals advising me I could very easily die if I did so.

I might have chosen to ignore both my clinicians and my body in favour of attempting to further my education, but in the days that followed, I learned that my health – or lack thereof – would have more of an impact on my life than a 2:1 from a middling university. Crohn's disease is a type of inflammatory bowel disease. Little is known about it, but many classify the illness as an autoimmune condition. In short, my digestive system views itself as a foreign object it should attack. Severity of the condition varies, but my symptoms include abdominal pain, low energy, and a general feeling of having no idea what is going on with my bowels. It's unknown why people contract Crohn's. It's not easily pinpointed to one specific trigger; anything from unlucky genes to stress, a food group, lack of sleep or an internal bodily reaction can set the disease in motion.

During the first couple of years of my life as a chronically ill woman, I refused to believe my condition would be any more prominent in my life than a minor inconvenience. Despite hospital stays, medication changes and multiple specialist appointments, despite having to inject myself with immunosuppressants, suffering extreme joint pain and debilitating fatigue, I set about my predetermined plans as if nothing had happened. When approaching life with such extreme denial and tunnel vision, the void seemed further away than ever before.

I discovered very quickly that the problem with ignoring something is that it doesn't make it disappear. While I remained clear on the direction I wished my life to take, my body had different plans. Quantifiably, as the months ticked by, my condition was improving: inflammatory markers derived from blood tests were down, my stomach was healing itself from the inside, and I was being tapered off the steroids that bloated my face. But moving from university to the working world, I was faced with the realisation that my Crohn's disease wouldn't diminish just because I willed it to.

The more the disease settled into my body, the more

I realised my symptoms wouldn't budge. I would spend hours staring at a screen, completely overcome by brain fog that refused to dissipate despite looming deadlines. Required to spend long days at my desk, I found myself instead locked in the staff loo, doubled over in pain and unable to move. As my symptoms became more and more prevalent, anxiety mounted, and the thought of entering the office each day filled me with dread.

I left my dream job due to my employers being unable to adapt my position to accommodate my illness. Through a combination of my inability to work a normal nine-to-five and my body's insistence on shutting down, which forced me to sleep for a few hours in the middle of the day, my condition was met with gross misunderstanding from the majority of people I came into contact with. Piece by piece, the vision I'd conjured of what my adult life would look like began to fall apart.

Following the early years of my diagnosis, I began to make sense of what the void meant to me. If anything, it has become increasingly tangible for me, as the void exists inside my body as a muddling mess of illness and unanswered questions. I've seen printed-out pictures of my own insides taken with cameras inserted down my throat, but I'm yet to be convinced there is little more behind my bones than a big black hole. I can feel my muscles cramping, but no matter the number of doctor's appointments I attend, I'm no closer to figuring out why they do.

For chronically ill people, the ability to ponder what all of this life stuff *means* is a luxury. To pause and consider our larger existence on this planet would require us to overlook our own internal, physical but invisible pain. Ignoring the void and refusing to acknowledge what often seems like the pointlessness of our existence is a means of survival. Left unchecked, I could spend hours burrowing into self-pity and self-loathing. For some, the concept of succumbing to the void is enough in and of itself to isolate them. But it is my body that separates me from the rest of the world, not my inability to find a meaningful place within it. To spend too much time searching inside myself for answers – whether with the help of medical professionals or independently – is to slip into the void, and to accept that my meaning will always be contingent on something I have no control over. The lack of clarity as to why my broken body refuses to heal itself is enough to incite a lifetime's worth of dread.

Perhaps my refusal to spend too much time considering the fragile nature of how my insides operate is another form of void-avoidance. It could be argued that my misunderstanding of why this uncertainty consumes so many of those around me isn't a misunderstanding at all, but a refusal to accept reality. While my own anxieties are projected internally onto myself, my void is fundamentally no different to those who feel engulfed by the largeness of the universe. Everyone has their issues. As I came to terms with my condition, I began ignoring my own internal bodily mess in favour of filling up my mind with other people's stories; consuming as much as I could about women's pain. I became convinced that if I armed myself with enough knowledge on the subject, I would find a way to be at peace with it.

Historically, the unwell have been written out of existence. Until recent history, it appeared near impossible to find an example of sickness, mental illness or those who don't fall into our narrow, Westernised beauty standards that wasn't focused on the negative stigma attached to those identity markers. With no positive role models to point towards, allowing yourself the kindness and consideration you would automatically apply to those around you is not an easy thing. In the case of chronic health conditions, this can largely be attributed to the wilful ignorance of the majority of able-bodied societies, or their outward insistence on ignoring those who are unwell. But we also have a part to play in our own invisibility. In the initial stages of my life as an ill woman, I led myself to believe that my condition was not worthy of any outward head space. My internalised ableism ensured I never spoke more than a whisper about what I was going through. My insistence on refuting the void kept me tight-lipped when discussing my own personal experiences.

In contrast, social politics and fourth-wave feminism have defined my early twenties. I came of age with the internet. I've witnessed the explosion of body positivity, self-care and a wider understanding of identity politics into our everyday lexicon. The internet was the first place I turned to when looking for answers about my condition. I spent hours searching social media networks for tips and tricks on how to cope when muddling through the world felt impossible. I can attribute all of my favourite films, bands, designers and artists to an obsession with seeking things out online. Before feminism became fodder for the advertising industry, logging on to my laptop felt like accessing a portal to another universe, one in which people with experiences similar to my own didn't feel choked by facets of themselves that traditionally made them weak.

After spending my teenage years lurking behind a keyboard, post-diagnosis I was able to mobilise those years spent on my laptop fangirling into confidence that pushed me to find my own community and seek out the spaces I longed to see in the world. With the internet and social media allowing marginalised people total autonomy over their stories – perhaps for the first time in modern history – our narratives have never been easier to disseminate across the world. With a focus on greater representation resulting in a more equal world, my generation's activism pushes for acceptance of our differences. Both online and in real life, my peer group has cultivated the ability to find common ground within the aspects of ourselves that have traditionally forced us to feel isolated.

When much of your time is spent housebound due to

unbearable pain, life online has a funny way of swallowing you up, for better or for worse. While I found great comfort in immersing myself in online communities during the first years of my diagnosis, spending so much time on the internet has become infinitely more confusing as the end of my twenties creep towards me. In recent years, sociopolitical activism has steered its focus towards greater representation for marginalised identities. While collective action grouped my peers and me together as I came of age, individual recognition is now the driving motivation for many currently operating in online spaces.

As someone with an invisible illness, representation can seem like an impossible plight. While there is huge comfort to be derived from seeing others being openly, unapologetically themselves, things become more complicated when the very thing that marginalises you is largely impossible for anyone else to see. For every time I have found a genuine community, a cynical URL 'girl gang' is peddling social hierarchy under the guise of uplifting other femmes. For every phrase adopted to help those ignored within popular culture, capitalism finds a way to use the very thing that brought you comfort to sell you back insecurity.

Once upon a time, existing online felt like belonging to a secret club of similar experience. Now, the new ilk of identity politics is a language we all speak. This democratisation of the tools and words that seek to empower us is largely a positive thing. It's created a means for us all to express the frustrations that come with a lifetime of feeling invisible. However, the popularity of social politics in the online world has let consumerist endeavours steal the coping mechanisms many of us spent our formative years figuring out. Those who sought greater acceptance on the internet during their teens have grown up to realise that being more visible does not automatically mean we are inciting real, meaningful change. At one point in my life the internet felt like holding a mirror up to myself, even if those I related to didn't directly experience the same things I did. Now, authenticity is even more difficult to determine online than in physical spaces. The mirrors we all seek in order to assert who we are have become distorted. Where the internet used to be a safe haven to dispel the creeping omnipresence of the void in my existence, the pressure to live our best life has cultivated an online world that reflects the outer world's murky value system.

Although my physical sense of personhood may feel constantly in flux, my sense of what is important has only been cemented by living as a person with Crohn's disease. The freedom I've found from being a medically confirmed sick sad girl is almost equal to the restrictions I experience in terms of my illness. After spending the first portion of my life riddled with self-doubt, being diagnosed with an incurable medical condition has had a funny way of teaching me to not give a fuck. For every person that dismissed my diagnosis due to its invisibility, I became more and more certain that playing down its effect on my life was doing more harm than good. For every wilfully ignorant comment that looped in my mind, I became determined to push my perceived flaws – my illness, my fatness, my mental insta-bility – onto the world as facets of humanity that should be not just accepted, but loved and adored. While I might lament the hours spent tucked up under the covers, unable to move and in isolation from my peers, the void did not rear its ugly head.

My invisible illness has willed me to ask for more from my circumstances than I was offered. Crohn's disease has pushed me to carve a place for myself in a world that negates my existence and demands optimum productivity, while rewarding peak wellness. My condition allows me to view both the on- and offline world with a fierce cynicism, while pushing me to constantly find the brightness within it. To move away from a void that lives within you is essen-tially an impossible task. It's easy to feel dispensable when your identity is intertwined with illness. You move through your life as a personification of the thing many people fear will happen to them one day. But to embrace a condition that by default makes you undesirable to the majority of our society holds an inherent power. To take back the parts of yourself you've learned to bury opens up a world of infinite possibility.

As I wade through adult life, my ability to accept the

void that is my body strengthens. Piece by piece, I'm learning that we're worthy of writing ourselves back into our own stories – and that history can no longer afford to ignore us.

The tragic and gorgeous history of the sick girl

To be unwell is to be the living and breathing epitome of what will eventually come for us all: the end of our lives.

Like death, illness fascinates society in a perverse way. We never want to experience its effects ourselves, but can't look away from those who do.

Nobody wants to be sick. More often than not, we do as much as we can to avoid it. We cower from people who cough on public transport, avoid making doctor's appointments, and push health concerns to the side for months on end until it's no longer possible to ignore them. It's understandable: being ill isn't fun. It ruins our plans and makes us feel like shit. But beyond the physical symptoms, we're taught that getting sick is a sign of weakness, and to become unwell is to lose our usefulness to society. If you're a marginalised person, this is a particularly unsettling thought, with our place in the world seeming fragile at even the best of times. The idea of being permanently unwell becomes even more unappealing when we realise that chronically ill and disabled people are treated with a near-total disregard for their existence.

Unwell and disabled people move through a world that has no interest in accommodating us. Only 60 out of 270 London Tube stations have partial accessibility; there are only nine hundred public toilets for a population of nearly 9 million in the same city; and when it comes to clothing, there are more options for dogs than there are for people with disabilities. Being sick is also embarrassing; it implies you cannot care for yourself to the standard that other people manage to, that your body is out of control, and that if your illness is contagious, you are happy to spread disease among others.

Our idea of sickness is explicitly tied up with fear. Initially, a fear of being unwell stems from the worry of embarrassing ourselves. Nobody wants to throw up in public, have to run to a toilet, sweat excessively, or say they're unable to climb a flight of stairs. But this embarrassment is merely a mask for something darker. The fear we feel about illness and all its associated symptoms directly correlates to the idea that not only does being unwell reduce quality of life, it closes the gap between life and death. To be unwell is to be the living and breathing epitome of what will eventually come for us all: the end of our lives. In extreme cases, the idea that you should even be alive as a disabled or chronically ill person is called into question by the people you love the most, as if you're a wounded baby animal begging to be put down. But for some of us, sickness isn't a choice, and we can't opt out. There is no avoiding the fear, disgust and contempt many people have for us. There is no avoiding the looming fear that our lives may be cut short. Being perpetually unwell is something we have to live with.

When I was first diagnosed with Crohn's disease, it felt like I was the only person in the world who was experiencing facing the rest of their life as an unwell person. Of course, I had heard about sick people before. But these tales were usually packaged within the context of terminal conditions, or those reaching the later stages of their life, in which health complications are more common and seem further away. The stories of those diagnosed when young always had tragic endings, and alluded to a short, sharp and sudden decline in health. The first few weeks, months and even years after diagnosis were extremely lonely. Not because I didn't have the support of those around me, but because I didn't know anyone else who was experiencing anything remotely similar to what I was going through.

No matter how many hours I spent googling my condition, stalking forums and joining Facebook groups, I still felt completely isolated. I had no idea what a person like me looked like or how they lived their lives. It seemed impossible that we could have ambitions beyond merely existing, that we could achieve our dreams, have successful careers or happy families. For a while, it felt as though my life would spiral into irrelevance, with my sole concerns being dictated by a disease I had no power over. The reason why stories of women suffering from illness and invisible disability are so few and far between is not because they don't exist.

Every year, 33,000 people are newly diagnosed with Crohn's disease, with over four million people in the UK living with autoimmune diseases, a statistic that is thought to be underreported. Crohn's disease is more prevalent in women, with autoimmune diseases in general being twice as likely to affect women as their male counterparts. The precise reasons for this imbalance are still unknown, as is so much about the nature of autoimmune conditions. But theories point towards our increased hormonal shifts and an additional X chromosome, meaning women's genetic make-up leaves us more prone to developing a tendency for our bodily cells to attack themselves.

Over the course of the COVID-19 pandemic, we have all experienced the fear of becoming unwell, and we are now seeing an entire new population of chronically ill people – those living with long COVID. However, despite the fact that vast swathes of us are experiencing disease to varying degrees, illness still persists as an extreme modern taboo. A taboo that leads many women who deal with chronic health conditions to refuse to talk about or acknowledge them altogether. More than simply feeling uncomfortable when the topic arises, we often aim to keep our illnesses hidden for as long as possible. Admitting you're unwell and openly talking about your condition leaves you extremely vulnerable; people take you less seriously, believe you're incapable, and overwhelm you with a sympathy you never wanted.

Growing up as part of Generation Overshare, with easy internet access and my peers writing their every thought and feeling in blog posts, I initially struggled to understand the resistance to openly admitting a long-term medical condition. I came of age believing that the act of simply talking about the things that held us back would help us progress into a more equal society. However, I quickly learned this was not the case. To talk about illness, about all the disgusting things that happen both inside and because of your body, is to allow people to be openly fearful of your existence.

Well people, once you admit you are sick, will spend the duration of your relationship tiptoeing around you, whether they consciously realise it or not. Though this reaction isn't necessarily malicious, the fact that we don't know how to behave around sick people reinforces our negative societal feelings about those who are unwell, and perpetuates fear through silence, further isolating those who live with health conditions. As I became more used to being sick, I began to hide my condition more frequently. Not because I was embarrassed, but because I was tired of how others responded to my admission. Disclosing every blood test, hospital visit or intrusive test would unwittingly invite either a barrage of questions relating to every scientific detail of my symptoms, or a pitying stare and pat on the back that would make me feel no more respected than a toddler.

Considering how society treats those who are sick, it's unsurprising that women in the spotlight who live with ongoing illness are often secretive about their conditions. Determined to find role models who didn't fall into the category of SHEOs, models-turned-activists or wellness gurus, I embarked on an all-encompassing mission to find women whose experiences mirrored my own more closely. After hours and hours spent exploring the cultural crevices of online listicles, obscure books and the deepest depths of Netflix, I started to access a world in which I was no longer alone.

I can now list every household name in the last century who has experienced chronic health conditions – for example, John F. Kennedy and Kurt Cobain both had Crohn's disease. I can recall every cultural artefact with a marginal connection to illness, like the fact that *Alien* (1979) is supposedly inspired by the writer's experience with Crohn's, with the alien itself representing the extreme, squirming nature of stomach pain. But what I learned about how society treats those who are in the spotlight while also being chronically ill was far from encouraging. While I managed to find what I was looking for, it became clear that representation of famous women's illnesses is largely either diminished or romanticised.

Those who buy a Frida Kahlo tea towel or sofa cushion may never become aware of the multiple surgeries, complications and periods of ill health she dealt with throughout her life. The Mexican artist has become a symbol for female empowerment, with her thick monobrow serving as a fuck-you to beauty standards, her countless self-portraits – a precursor to our modern obsession with the self – and the fact that she is probably one of the few female artists most people know by name. While our love for Kahlo may come from a vaguely political place, the reality of her existence has become completely sanitised, with her icon status eclipsing the real reasons we should love her in the first place.

Conversely, people who are aware of her personal history are quick to paint her as a woman riddled with disease and using art as the only escape from her sad existence. Kahlo was diagnosed with polio at age six, which caused her chronic pain throughout her life. At eighteen years old, she was in a bus accident, leading to multiple injuries. She spent months in bed, and underwent over thirty surgeries to treat various complications. The accident and its subsequent aftershocks also affected her fertility, and she experienced multiple miscarriages. Spending so much time bedridden and alone, she adapted her easel to accommodate her condition, with a mirror propped appropriately so she could paint herself. Creating work provided Kahlo with an opportunity to separate herself from the pain of her life, while representing her experiences and trauma.

Walking around a recent London exhibition featuring the artist's wardrobe, accessories and personal items, I came to realise just how pitied Kahlo still is despite all her success. As I moved through rooms showcasing her make-up compacts displayed next to medical devices and the plaster corsets she had to wear for much of her life, her wedding dress alongside medicine bottles, it became obvious that once people see illness, they struggle to see anything else. Hearing how others spoke about her in whispers was a jarring experience. While I saw inspiring resilience and creativity, many attendees at the exhibition regarded her as a woman whose suffering came to define her. Pity, in the visitor's eye, overwhelmed above all else.

It is tempting to view Kahlo as someone who triumphed in spite of the many physical barriers in her way. But in reality, the reason she was able to create such iconic work was because of her illness, not in spite of it. Her experiences with pain allowed an insight into femininity that her peers did not possess, handing her a unique set of perspectives that resonate among many of us regardless of health status. Instead of romanticising her ability to push through the pain, we should try to understand how it informed and shaped her work as much as any other part of her life – for better or for worse.

While Kahlo's history of illness is well documented, other famous women are less willing to embrace their condition as part of their creative process. Kathleen Hanna, riot grrrl pioneer and frontwoman of Bikini Kill, hid her Lyme disease diagnosis from the world, choosing to vanish into near obscurity while dealing with the condition. In the following years, during her return to public life, she did begin to open up about the effect of the disease on her well-being, but mostly in the context of missed tours and lost opportunities as opposed to the physical and emotional turmoil of living with illness. Similarly, Lady Gaga only spoke about her experiences with fibromyalgia in 2017, just before the release of her Netflix documentary. In the film, we watch her writhe around on sofas due to extreme pain, visit doctors and receive treatments. While this is a rare example of someone famous allowing the public candid access to her pain, in the years following the documentary, her fibromyalgia has been largely forgotten and rarely mentioned.

On one of my many evenings early on in my diagnosis spent typing 'famous people with Crohn's disease' and 'celebrities with chronic health conditions' into search bars, I discovered that Shannen Doherty, star of *Beverly Hills, 90210, Charmed* and *Heathers*, kept her Crohn's disease a secret for decades as it wasn't considered very sexy. This is a sentiment also echoed by writer Chris Kraus, who, while more forthcoming about her experience with Crohn's in her autobiographical novel *I Love Dick*, describes it as a disease that ultimately left her not only undesirable, but repulsive to her husband. Neither Kraus nor Doherty is inaccurate: Crohn's disease isn't sexy. Most people can't think of anything less appealing than dealing with a partner who could shit the bed at any moment and spends a huge proportion of their time in agony.

With a woman's worth still so hugely being placed on how much sex appeal she possesses, the only way to retain any relevance to patriarchal society is to lie about vast swathes of our lives, and conceal everything from cosmetic surgery to chronic illness. Our fear of being unsexy in the context of illness feeds all the way back to the fact that ultimately we consider unwell people to be a burden on society. No matter their talent or artistic genius, being sick is to be about as useless to the world as you can get. People feel undesirable for all sorts of reasons, but above most else, this fear of undesirability stems from a fear of rejection – something unwell people experience jarringly frequently in many forms and manners. We live with the fear of being rejected by those we love, denied care from our support networks and cast aside onto a pile of people deemed unworthy of love.

In relation to the endless list of ways in which women are expected to adapt their behaviour to fit the perfect vision of femininity constructed by men, creating an identity around sexual desirability has never been a personal priority. Early on in my life, at a time when most young women experience their sexual awakening, I realised I would never be a conventional vamp. My ability to project an aura of mystique has always been practically non-existent; I'm too loud, too fat, and incapable of keeping a secret for longer than five minutes. But though I've never spent too long agonising over my ability to seduce, I do feel immense guilt for putting the people I love through illness via osmosis.

There are some people we can't hide our conditions from. Eventually, the romantic partners Doherty chose would have had to find out about her Crohn's, even when her production teams did not, and in the end, she did disclose her condition to the world. I've been with my partner since I was fifteen. We've grown up with each other through school, university, first jobs and into adulthood, but the one thing he didn't sign up for was being lumbered with a perpetually sick person. As much as my life revolves around my condition, so does his, from every hospital appointment, to the days I'm too unwell to leave my bed and the constantly changing lists of diagnoses and medication. It's not an ideal way to spend your twenties, even if the experience is second-hand.

But although he has seen me in the most viscerally ugly and physically repulsive states I could possibly inhabit, the alternative is personally a far more scary option. Trading desirability for the opportunity to be truly understood and accepted is an easy decision. No matter my own guilt, I have to accept that he does not resent me for being unwell. That looking after me when I need care is not a burden, and that I am worth more than an abstract set of requirements equating to the right kind of woman. While Kraus's condition may not have been sexually appealing, she recalls within her book's pages how it did help her ensnare her then husband, Sylvère, with his desire to help her evolving into infatuation. Their love, to the outside eye, seems more pragmatic than led by a burning passion. They married so she could be added to his healthcare plan, and he was the only person able to talk her out of the emotional despair that resulted from a physical flare-up.

Their story taught me that not all great love affairs require drama or mystery. Every sick girl needs at least one person whose behaviour never veers into condescending pity or refusal to accept reality. Who won't openly wish they could help you get better and instead simply accepts the fact that your pain is a part of life. It still makes me cringe every time my Crohn's disease results in something traditionally embarrassing. I may not be able to control the outside judgement and projected perception from peers, colleagues, friends or family. I equally can't curb the pangs of guilt every time I cancel on someone, or upset them, or watch my boyfriend wash the dishes for the ten millionth time because I'm in too much pain to do so.

But to lie to my partner, or anybody else, about the reality of my condition would mean shrinking myself for the sole purpose of appearing palatable. Not only that, but it would mean closing myself off from the opportunity to really see the best in people. Yes, unwell people are treated like shit a lot of the time. But most of this ill-will comes from a societal stigma and not a personal hatred. Experiencing all of my sick little life alongside my boyfriend has shown me that people can truly be unwavering when it comes to love. That humans are capable of caring completely, and unselfishly. That the people around us really are willing to experience the worst of times with you alongside the best. If I chose to lie about or underplay my condition, I would live with the constant fear that if people found out the truth of my existence, I'd end up totally alone.

The less we speak about our illnesses, the more we allow outside perception to dictate truth. Silence allows others to tell our stories, to decide what a sick person does or does not look like, and declare whose experiences are important and whose should be ignored. It remains rare to see a representation of illness that lays bare the often-ugly reality of existing as an abnormality, that resists the categorisation of either waif or powerhouse, helpless beauty or force of nature, because we still allow the patriarchy, and non-disabled people, to dictate the right type of unwell woman. Those who do open up about their experiences are subjected to an infantilisation that often ensures they stay silent beyond those initial overshares. But beyond being babied, women who remain unfiltered in the telling of their lives are often regarded as unhinged, inappropriate and out of control.

Some of us choose to lean into this, with Kraus describing her Crohn's disease as 'hysteria of the organs', and explicitly correlating her irritable bowel disease flaring up with her mental health declining. But being labelled as 'confessional' or frequently being told we are oversharing when discussing illness are uncomfortable descriptors often placed upon us against our will. Why should asserting the very real things we go through be considered a confession?

After recovering from cancer, losing her bladder (among other organs) and learning that she would have to live the rest of her life with a urostomy bag, artist Tracey Emin began taking nude selfies documenting her changing body. On publication of the images, the artist told the *Guardian* that she refuted the confessional label, and the implication that freely speaking about her life – urostomy bag and all – constituted a performance.

Emin's work has always laid bare the reality of womanhood, whether it be heartbreak, sexuality or now illness. Her work is highly personal and was considered confessional long before her cancer diagnosis. The fact that people believe her symptoms to be amped up for the purpose of art is just one example of how we still consider any woman who speaks about her experiences with her body to be making an unnecessary fuss. In reality, we have always been wary of any femme who seeks to disrupt the cis-patriarchal status quo and anyone who pushes past taboos in order to break them down. We are still slowly unpicking centuries of women being told to be quiet and to put up with the things that harm us. But where – in liberal circles at least – there has been increased acceptance of discussion surrounding periods, sadness or the fact that women are in fact sexual beings, illness still shocks people.

Deep down, we would prefer that sick people keep their pain to themselves and not remind us that one day we could be in their position too. Unwell women live with their symptoms every day. We live with every pang of pain, every day spent in bed, every burst ulcer in our stomach and every subsequent surgery. Sharing these experiences, whether at work, in online spaces or among friends, should be no more shocking than revealing that you have a hangover or a cold. That we still regard discussing the physicality of illness as something to feel guilty about only speaks to the fact that we consider every other person in the world before we consider those who are sick. That we prioritise well people's comfort over the need for unwell people to feel seen, understood and acknowledged in a world that would prefer to ignore us.

On the rare occasion we can stomach discussion of illness, it is fed to us through a voyeuristic gaze. Over the last decade, across film and TV, we have become infatuated with fictionalised unwell women. Two types of illness are most commonly found on our screens in these tales: the fragile young woman who needs the love of a good boy to see her through the final stage of her life; and the twisted, evil, not-really-ill-but-definitely-mentally-unstable girl tackling Munchausen's syndrome or Munchausen's by proxy. The former for a while in the 2010s came to replace traditional teen films. *The Fault in Our Stars*, *Me and Earl and the Dying Girl*, *Babyteeth*, *Five Feet Apart* and *Midnight Sun* all deal with terminally ill teens finding love in the last months of their life. While *The Politician*, *The Act*, *Sharp Objects*, *Everything*, *Everything*, *Ma* and *Phantom Thread* all tell stories of young women being tricked into illness by someone close to them.

Their plot points might seem miles apart but the overall message is the same: unwell people are helpless, lacking in autonomy, and need to be rescued. In the case of our teen cancer buddies, the message is that a life doomed to be cut short is not a life worth living; that is, until they meet a boy able to change their mind. Or even worse, these female characters represent a sort of distorted manic pixie dream girl, whose tragic existence teaches our male protagonist that there really is more to life than his own small-minded problems. Her thoughts, feelings and pain are reduced to a plot that does no more than provide a lesson in growth for a man not yet in his twenties; she exists only to give agency to his story.

Munchausen's narratives frame illness as the worst possible thing to happen to someone, showing us characters being stripped of their power, force-fed drugs and tricked into surgeries they don't need. While both tropes veer into trauma porn, these plots frame illness as a weapon – something that can be used against a person at any moment to make them utterly powerless in the world. Such stories are nearly always told from the position of an onlooker, never the unwell person or those experiencing sickness by proxy. They are largely concerned with how the ill character's behaviour affects those around them, rather than the implications of living as a person with disease.

Our films about terminally ill teens romanticise illness; they paint it as something that is cruel and painful but that also elevates the emotions and feelings of the characters. Those featuring Munchausen's or Munchausen's by proxy demonise being unwell, with many of our heroines killing, torturing, or enacting acts of violence as a by-product of being forced into illness. Both genres are tragic; they largely feature young, conventionally beautiful women who are presented as deserving better from the world than the symptoms they are grappling with. Neither story, no matter how they are told, represents the true spectrum of illness, but instead amplifies the same damaging stereotypes we've been fed throughout modern history.

Picture a sickly girl in your head: she likely has long, flowing hair, pale skin and an extremely slim figure, and perhaps is even wearing a white nightgown. This visual stereotype is not an accident, but rather has been carefully crafted across centuries. We imagine unwell women as mysterious and sad, weak, submissive and unable to care for themselves – and we always imagine them through the patriarchal gaze. Like death, illness fascinates society in a perverse way. We never want to experience its effects ourselves, but we can't look away from those who do. Despite our disgust towards those who currently live with disability, the trope of the unwell woman has long been depicted as a source of desire across art, literature, film and more.

The unsettling yet romanticised link between sick women, death and lust has long persevered within our society, with these stereotypical origins dating back as far as the 1800s. Edgar Allen Poe once declared the death of a beautiful woman as 'unquestionably the most poetic topic in the world'. Following the deaths of his mother, his wife and practically every other woman he knew, the writer aimed to transform his grief into something less devastating, reframing sadness as euphoric and death as a beautiful act.

Poe wasn't the only author who sought to romanticise illness, with many writers during the Romantic era of the 1800s framing sickness – in particular tuberculosis – as something caused by an excess of passion. With notable authors such as John Keats and Elizabeth Barrett Browning dying from the illness, creatives of all mediums aimed to redefine their suffering as something enviable, aspirational and important. As the bodies of great creative minds literally began piling up, a myth emerged that their genius was actually caused by their illness, with symptoms of tuberculosis being thought to elevate the mind's capabilities.

But the impact and influence of this romanticisation of illness extends far beyond words on a page, transcending the singular diagnosis of tuberculosis and permeating our beauty standards right up to this day. Physical manifestations of tuberculosis include weight loss leading to extreme skinniness, and the colour draining from your skin. But despite these features indicating a life-ending disease, healthy women of the era began to mimic the aesthetic, chemically whitening their skin and starving themselves to get the consumptive look. This beauty standard was pioneered by Elizabeth Siddal, the model in Pre-Raphaelite painting *Ophelia* by Sir John Everett Millais.

Siddal, despite being an artist in her own right, became a muse for a number of the movement's painters, and her stint as Ophelia left her with pneumonia that led to a life-time of health problems. Thought to have suffered from tuberculosis herself, and often described as beautiful and fragile, she turned the tide on what attractiveness meant in the nineteenth century, steering beauty standards away from rounder bodies towards tall and skinny ones, and shifting red hair from being considered the pinnacle of ugliness to the height of seduction. While her mental health struggles – and the fact that she lost her life to suicide – are more widely accepted and discussed, her physical disabilities have defined our expectations of what female sickness looks like.

Our societal obsession with tall, skinny, pale women is as intoxicating now as it was then, but although our attitude towards what we consider beautiful ebbs and flows, our image of the archetypal unwell woman remains the same. She is pictured as something in the world's past, a sad victim of a period in which medicine wasn't advanced and women were locked up in institutions for speaking their minds. We may now have doctors and care teams to manage the minute details of our conditions, but the idea of unwell women is still the same as it was then: we must be beautiful, fragile and submissive.

This frozen-in-time depiction of what it looks like to suffer long-term illness is no doubt damaging to the millions of women who live with chronic health conditions. However, I understand the desire to romanticise your life. I've taken selfies from hospital beds, and crafted (and then deleted) long, self-pitying Instagram captions pertaining to the details of my Crohn's disease. I've daydreamed from my sickbed that I am in fact a Renaissance-era muse, rather than a grotty young woman who's refused to change her clothes in days and who hasn't been able to muster the energy to take a shower. Just like the artists engulfed in the consumption epidemic, I fantasise that my illness serves a greater purpose as a coping mechanism. It's easier to accept my reality by believing that everything has great meaning, rather than falling into the existential dread of understanding that I've just been dealt an unlucky hand in life.

While the modern poor little sick girl may not have paintings hung in prestigious galleries, we have another tool at our fingertips: social media. Our desire to seek external validation for the things we experience internally has grown exponentially since the advent of the internet, and those who are ill are not immune to the seduction of sharing every detail with those who follow us. The hashtag #hospitalselfies contains over 50,000 images, largely of young women posing from their hospital beds. Online communities and Instagram accounts chronicling the experience of chronically ill and disabled women rack up tens of thousands of followers. For perhaps the first time in history, we have the opportunity to control our own narratives.

Like Emin and Kraus, we can overshare to our heart's content. We can also connect more easily than ever before with those who share similar experiences. But whether this oversharing really benefits our lives beyond racking up likes and Insta-attention is unclear. On the one hand, it is now practically impossible to shut out unwell and disabled people. Where our image has historically been controlled by those who would rather ignore our existence, we now have the opportunity to tell the truth and force ourselves to be visible in online forums. However, for every enlightening Instagram caption and vital support group, there are hundreds of posts countering these steps forward with harmful rhetoric that further ensures that unwell women are only accepted if they fall into an easily understood binary. The new era of romanticising illness is online, for better and for worse.

Social media, at its core, is voyeuristic, and encourages us to share the best parts of ourselves. This creates an uncomfortable tension – we're sharing more about our lived experiences, but through rose-tinted glasses in a plea to be adored by people who are fundamentally terrified of becoming us. A hospital gown becomes a fashion moment, boxes of pills a perfect still life, and vaccinations provide the perfect opportunity for a selfie. While this does go some way towards destigmatisation, we are still more concerned with presenting ourselves as palatable than being accepted warts and all. Romanticising your existence in online spaces provides the illusion of progress without breaking down any barriers outside of the online world. It allows well people to feel as though they couldn't possibly hate us while continuing to mistreat and judge unwell people when encountering them offline.

We still experience workplace discrimination, get caught short when looking for public bathrooms, and face misunderstanding from nearly everyone in our lives. Supportive comments and likes that stretch into the hundreds may feel good in the moment, but they do little to improve our lives long-term. Social media, at its worst, also warps illness into something weirdly aspirational, just like the teen cancer on-screen dramas. It scrapes the most tragically gorgeous parts of our experiences without urging anyone to interrogate more deeply. We finally have an opportunity to be the main character, and to shine a light on our experiences of illness without reservation. But still this freedom is only reserved for those who can remain unthreatening enough to garner the adoration of those who are well. This new-found visibility is both frustrating and liberating, maddening and relieving. I no longer feel alone, but navigating the modern world, and the way I am perceived as a chronically ill woman within it, feels infinitely complicated.

More often than not, I resist the urge to seek health-related attention online. There are limits to how often unwell people should be expected to openly embrace and proudly declare their conditions, no matter how tempting it is to garner some easy validation with a snap of my daily medication. In reality, these admissions via posts that only capture people's attention for seconds often result in negative repercussions away from social media. The pay-off from posting a compromising selfie rarely feels worth it in the long run. For every time my desire to casually overshare feels like a desperate thirst, I remember the moments in which being open about my illness has come back to bite me. These posts also feed into the voyeurism that drives our parasocial obsession with strangers' lives; we feel like we understand each other without any of the actual work and empathy required to truly treat unwell people with the respect they deserve.

Despite the fact that I live every single day in pain, my symptoms are as familiar to me as any other regular aspect of my existence. So much so that nearly a decade on from diagnosis, I barely pay them a second thought. Living with stomach pain is something I rarely even acknowledge as I go about my day. Yes, I am probably in pain while you're talking to me, my stomach is almost definitely in knots while we're eating dinner, and I am most likely weighing up how long it will take me to reach the bathroom if necessary. However, having this externally validated through the near-constant questioning of others – both online and off – somehow feels more real than the constant rumbling of my digestive system. While I've come to accept the reality of what a day feels like for me, the constant poking and prodding serves as a reminder that in their eyes I will always be different.

Watching people constantly sharing infographics pertaining to the rights of disabled people with no further interrogation or interest into our actual lived experience is depressing, and does little to make me feel more accepted. My life often seems like a double-edged sword: openly talk about my condition in the hope of living a better-understood existence, or minimise it in the hope of being treated like a normal human being. This becomes even more of a complicated thought when paired with the fact that I so desperately sought representation in those first few years of diagnosis and struggled to find any. I can understand why, for so many women, hidden illness is their dirty little secret.

For huge swathes of those who live with illness, hiding their disabilities isn't an option. However, having the choice between concealment and honesty is no walk in the park. We need to find a way forward in which representation isn't a trap. While we continue to box unwell women into stereotypes that discourage people from coming forward with their experiences, we need to move beyond only accepting feminine sickness when we can either romanticise it or pity it.

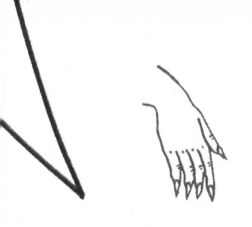

The nail shop

The word self-care is so familiar to us
all that it is almost entirely meaningless –
and as frivolous as the monthly trips
I take to get my nails done.

The feeling of having my nails drilled with
tiny yet lethal tools, followed by a thick
plastic paste and slick of bright red polish
applied to the top of my fingertips, left me
more relaxed than any guided meditation,
yoga class or good night's sleep.

What is and what is not self-care is a discourse that has birthed a thousand memes, from satire to self-serving, well-meaning and ridiculous. Self-care is a bubble bath; self-care is also brushing your teeth when you're depressed. It's taking no shit, and also abandoning all responsibility and moving to an abandoned forest where no one can find you. If you've logged on to the internet, turned on the television or spoken to another human being in the last ten years, you've probably stumbled across the concept. Even for those who don't live in the same corner of the internet as I do, the idea of self-care has become shorthand for prioritising your own well-being by whatever means necessary.

I stumbled upon the concept of self-care in my late teens. Scouring the internet for anything that might make me feel better either physically or psychologically, I was met with a wall of social media posts and personalities teaching their followers that looking after yourself is one of the most important things a person can do. The advice was wide-ranging; from Audre Lorde quotes artfully typed in beautiful fonts accompanied by activist sentiments, to suggested skincare routines and how to masturbate. These posts were probably the first instance in which I encountered the idea of your personal identity being informed by and aligned with your political beliefs beyond actual government. I learned that the way I treat myself should not only be reflective of my morals, but that self-care was thought of among my peers as something that could actually make you a better person.

The concept was presented to me neatly in a package of fourth-wave feminist thought cultivated online. It sat alongside other easily understood slogans along the lines of *teenage girls will change the world, femmes to the front,* and *the way I dress does not mean yes* – catchy slogans that make you feel inspired enough to like or repost to your own feed. But not all of the content was frivolous; the first things I learned about boundaries, anxiety and depression were all discovered through the lens of self-care. In some ways, post-diagnosis, through university and into my first job, the simple notion that drilled itself into all of our brains came to play a vital role in my decision-making – in both serious and stupid ways. If completing my daily tasks would make me more unwell, avoiding them could be written off as self-care. Spending a ridiculous amount of money on a new outfit when I'd had a bad body day was part of prioritising my own happiness in the name of self-care. My ability to check in with my own feelings in social situations and find the confidence to reassess certain relationships stemmed from discovering self-care. Getting three takeaways in one day when hung-over was and still is my personal favourite form of self-care.

As my generation grew up from living teenage lives with teenage problems to paying bills, working long hours and dealing with adulthood, we felt lost. Or at least I did, with a chronic illness I barely understood biologically, let alone how it translated to changes in how I looked after myself practically or independently in a day-to-day sense. Thrust into the real world and faced with being overworked, barely paid, and having no down time, it's unsurprising that we sought new ways to self-soothe away from the comfort of our families, childhood friends and economic stability.

Initially, the idea that self-care is a radical political act integral to our individual and collective happiness sat mostly separate from the consumerist side of the internet. Learning about this stuff felt like resource sharing, rather than the online world we live in now, which targets us with every type of product we could ever wish for at each available moment.

But as the world itself became more volatile – politically, with Trump's 2016 election in the US and Brexit in the UK; environmentally, as the effects of climate change became increasingly obvious; and medically, as a major pandemic left us all trapped inside our homes – seemingly overnight, self-care grew in the collective consciousness. As not only young marginalised people but the entire Western global population teetered on the edge of major breakdowns, commerce swooped in, merging the political with capitalism and creating the mutated brand of self-care we all know and love to hate. Self-care has become shorthand for brands that wish to tag themselves onto the wellness trend and appear as though they care about their customers' mental health, with little further action required than sticking the sentiment onto the item of their choice. As with so much of fourth-wave feminism, the seeds that allowed these sentiments to mutate into marketing material were planted by young women seeking simply to make their lives more bearable – and I was one of them.

Despite my own cynicism towards brands that claim to care about how we feel, I am not immune to the irresistible allure of buying more stuff, jumping on a beauty fad, or loading up my face with every sheet mask going in an attempt to feel more human. The summer after being diagnosed with Crohn's disease, I began getting my nails done. After starting a course of steroids to tackle the flare-up in my stomach, my natural nails were ruined. The medication that was healing my insides was causing calcium deficiency and leaving me with brittle, breaking nails that had already withstood a lifetime of being bitten down the cuticle and having the surrounding skin pulled until it bled.

Before being chronically ill, I was never interested in spending any sort of time in a salon chair. I rarely had my hair cut, couldn't care less about waxing, and thought acrylic nails were a waste of time. My skincare routine until my mid-twenties barely even stretched to moisturiser, and make-up was sparingly used to outline my eyes with a thick black flick and otherwise left to rot at the bottom of my toiletry bag. While I did care about how I looked, I was afraid of appearing to try too hard, or making it too obvious that my femininity was in fact important to me. I spent most of my money on cheap clothes and box hair dyes that made me feel cool, but I could never justify dropping fifty pounds on a beauty treatment that felt temporary, fleeting and frivolous.

I'm not sure what changed in my brain in that summer after diagnosis, or what led me into the nail shop for the first time. Whether it was a desperate ploy to take back some semblance of control over a body that was trying to kill me or the fact that I'd spent a year at fashion school engrossed in every possible beauty or fashion trend is irrelevant. The feeling of having my nails drilled with tiny yet lethal tools, followed by a thick plastic paste and a slick of bright red polish, left me more relaxed than any guided meditation, yoga class or good night's sleep. Sitting in the chair, picking out crystals to adorn my nearly-too-long false talons, I felt a peace that was hard to replicate. Leaving the salon with a fresh set of acrylics provided a rush of endorphins that sustained me for days on end.

My body is an out-of-control beast, one that can't be curbed by strong will, medication or treatment plans. While my organs try to sabotage my existence from the inside, the least I can do is embellish my exterior with semi-ridiculous adornments in an attempt to feel better.

Whether my false nails are self-care, vanity or just a way to waste my time and money, I don't care; I have become utterly dependent on my manicurist.

These days the phrase 'self-care' is so familiar to us that it is almost entirely meaningless – and as frivolous as the monthly trips I take to get my nails done. We've seen make-up brands developing self-care collections and claiming that the right shade of lipstick or thickness of mascara brush can keep us grounded. TV programmes are developed entirely around the concept, with reality-show contestants urging us to close the social media apps that pay their bills and take a step back from the posts that make us feel bad about ourselves. There are annual national and international self-care weeks, in which our governments and health organisations peddle the techniques to help us look after ourselves rather than rely on their resources.

All of this would not be so offensive if our modern version of consumerist self-care actually worked. If all the scented candles, bath bombs, fancy face oils and fleeting breaks from burnout in the form of regular spa treatments actually made a tangible difference to our lives in a mean-ingful way; if we actually felt more at peace, and didn't spend our time searching for the next quick fix via a shop-ping spree, influencer or trend that promises to cure all our ills, then the argument for our current model of capitalist self-care would be an easier pill to swallow. The reality is that all of these conglomerates and influential individuals just want to make more money out of us, while asserting their intellectual and spiritual dominance in a field they actually have little understanding of.

But while they continue on their quest to raise their profit margins, self-care has become for many marginalised communities little more than an inside joke, a throwaway phrase spoken in the midst of making questionable decisions. The internet, made up of many fragmented pieces, seems to be divided into several different camps on the subject of what the practice looks like and means. On the one hand, there is the camp that still wholeheartedly and unironically believes in self-care's transformative powers, but in a highly individualistic, self-optimising way. These people post daily affirmations to their Instagram stories and bask in every self-care-related purchase they can get; they are essentially the 'live, laugh, love' mums of millennial culture. They're a well-meaning group, and if a fairly benign quote provides enough inspiration to help them get through the day, I am not one to judge. But this subset of people are equally the ones who are unlikely to scratch further beneath the surface of what effective self-care actually means to them on a personal or political level.

At the opposite end of the spectrum we have the hyperaware social media users who scroll down their Instagram feed smirking at each post as they double-tap. They've likely been around since self-care was first mentioned at the advent of fourth-wave feminism, but now they're over it.

They post satirical memes mocking the practice, and knowingly caption images of themselves spiralling downward or indulging in things that are stereotypically bad for you as self-care moments. In reality, this is the group that probably most deeply understands the true meaning of self-care, but the crassness of commodification has made them weary of engaging with it on any level apart from irony.

Then we have the wellness self-care warriors. For them, self-care may as well be another extension of diet culture. If you're not juicing, exercising daily and meditating as often as possible, then your self-care is invalid. They gleefully share every detail of their routine, from 4 a.m. workouts and acai bowls to supplements and energising infusions of pseudo-scientific potions backed up with absolutely no evidence that they make any positive difference to your health at all. To this group, self-care is another route to optimisation – to living their best lives and making sure everyone else follows and abides by their prescriptive rules when it comes to what constitutes being well.

In all cases, self-care has become something of an aspirational lifestyle choice rather than a necessary practice for yourself and your community. You're either too cool to care, open and self-accepting enough to post the intricacies of your vulnerabilities via pretty posts, or perfect enough to share everything you do so that others can yearn to live a life as impeccable as yours and seek to replicate these practices in their own lives.

Though all of these groups approach and think of self-care in vastly differing ways, they have one thing in common. We have all accepted that the practice of caring for ourselves has become inseparable from capitalism: buy more stuff, relieve yourself of the world's ills. The easiest way to feel better about yourself is to buy something that distracts you from the terror of existence. I didn't need self-care to teach me that. I understand the seduction of walking into a shop and falling in love with the perfect pair of shoes, a gorgeous bag or an incredible dress. I've stared at inanimate objects countless times and planned entire overhauls of my life around them, convinced that the way to move forward and become the person I want to be is entirely pinned on purchasing whichever item has caught my eye that week.

For much of my life, I haven't had the cash to make my extravagant, expensive dreams a reality, so I have become accustomed to treating myself in small ways to boost my serotonin. I make a habit of going for a nice meal or coffee after every hospital or doctor's appointment that doesn't require me to be escorted home by my next of kin. I buy myself small things when I'm having a bad week: a pair of cheap earrings, ridiculously impractical heels, or a vintage outfit on eBay that takes hours to hunt down. When I'm feeling well enough, I treat myself to fancy cocktails, take Ubers everywhere and get my nails done regularly, all in the name of self-care. Capitalism is hell, but small indulgences undoubtedly make life more bearable.

I'm not the only one who thinks this; in fact, it's scientifically proven. Despite the fact that we're all suddenly obsessed with experiences – booking holidays, visiting restaurants that go viral on TikTok, attending festivals and so on – research has found that buying new things sustains happiness over a longer period of time than going somewhere fun. Where the intensity of experiencing something unknown and exciting is deeply fulfilling for fleeting moments, buying the right products that are actually useful to us makes our lives easier for extended periods of time. But no matter how expensive your purchase is, unless that product has a longer, more meaningful lifespan than the random items of clothing and skincare procured during my 3 a.m. online spending sprees, the joy will fade.

Just as my nails grow out every four to six weeks, our ability to focus our attention on the existing objects in our lives is ever dwindling. We constantly lust after new things, as we see those we follow on the internet rotating a seemingly limitless wardrobe for selfies, capturing increasingly luxe homeware in still lives, and tweaking their physical appearance by undergoing whichever treatment is trending that week. The problem is, we do not only see these things once. The allure of caving and clicking 'checkout' would be easy to ignore if these tempting moments were just a tiny drop in the vast sea containing the millions of new posts generated every single day in the online world.

However, the algorithm ensures that once we've shown

an interest in practically anything buyable, we'll be bombarded with every iteration of that item for months to follow. Double-tap on a picture of a nice bag, or even just mention that you need a new bag while messaging a friend, and suddenly you'll start getting sponsored advertisements sprinkled between the posts made by your friends capturing their post-work Prosecco. Then, when reading an article online, the sidebar will be littered with accessory companies fighting for your attention and money. These little nudges towards the direction of parting with your cash will even haunt you in your email inbox as undercover ads.

When talking about bags, shoes or underwear, we all do possess the power to resist this onslaught, no matter how hard it feels at times. Prior to self-care, deep down it was obvious to all of us that the link between our spending habits and happiness was tenuous, frivolous and indulgent. Now, we're hyper aware that everything we own or interact with needs to serve us, and companies have cottoned on to the fact that we need more than a gorgeous-looking fabric or the perfect heel height to complete a purchase. They know that everything we let into our lives has to mean something, as well as contribute to our psychological well-being beyond the thrill of putting together the perfect outfit.

With conversations around mindful consumption, sustainability and the evil nature of corporations looming over us, we can no longer purchase things guilt free. That is, unless the item in question is going to contribute to our personal growth. We're sold tampons that not only do their job but claim to actually make our periods enjoyable and the whole experience a grounding exercise in mindfulness. Skincare is no longer for the purpose of only clearing our spots and delaying the ageing process, but for reconnecting with our physicality and finding peace after a stressful day. Our diaries are now 'wellness journals', in which we jot down gratitude lists next to our meetings and appointments.

Everything from socks and phone cases to art prints, throw cushions and jewellery is etched with little reminders for the outside world that you are committed to taking care of yourself. Swathes of lifestyle brands have managed to hinge their entire marketing calendar around the myth that their products are not superficial, while making absolutely no changes to ensure that the well-being of their staff, or the people who purchase their products, is prioritised. As long as they maintain the illusion of care, we are happy enough to continue purchasing more and more stuff and exchanging cash for the small buzz these items provide us with.

We are urged to believe that no matter how flawed or vague its messaging is, the corporate world has our best interests at heart. In reality, these companies have played a huge role in ensuring that self-care exists on the opposite side of the spectrum from what it once was:

community-based, revolutionised by social politics, and pushing back at a world that ostracises anybody who exists outside of social norms. Our mainstream approach to self-care is strikingly similar to the way we approach many facets of social politics: we have convinced ourselves that discussing it is the same as actually practising it. We have reached a point where we believe that solving huge injustices or issues is as simple as pointing out that they exist. Just as the media have dedicated periods of time to mental health awareness, in which we are all urged to speak about our issues with absolutely no infrastructure available to actually help us cope with them, we are taught that uttering the phrase 'self-care' is enough to make all our stress dissipate into irrelevance.

We associate self-care with the millennial experience, but the concept itself began as a medical one in the 1950s, with the first mentions of the philosophy dating way back to the ancient Greeks and the Romans. Developed by doctors to grant hospital inpatients and those receiving long-term treatment some autonomy over their health and bodies, self-care was first proposed as a way for extremely unwell people to regain control over the bodies that continuously disobeyed them, and to help those patients feel as though they had a hand in their medical treatment. Tasks such as brushing your own hair seem inane and obvious to most of us, though they do mirror the more patronising self-care checklists we see online that urge us to remember to wash our pants. However, for unwell people who spend twenty-four hours a day plugged into monitors, constantly talking to doctors and existing mainly within a hospital ward, these acts help remind them that they are human.

Initially, the idea of self-care was only relevant to those already unwell, but during the sixties, the philosophy behind it was widened, when a surge in academic interest in the effects of PTSD urged institutions to help those in high-pressure professions, flipping the script on the initial intended patients and refocusing self-care as a mindset applied to doctors, social workers and others in emotionally taxing jobs. This period in self-care's history focused on the idea that you are unable to meaningfully help anyone else if you are neglecting your own needs.

Within the next decade and into the seventies, the concept was adopted by civil rights activists, and shortly afterwards picked up by feminists. This caused self-care to break away from a purely medical definition and broaden out to focus on how healthcare and welfare systems ignored marginalised people, and what could be done to bridge the gap between living well and being discriminated against by public services and the government that presided over them. These groups redefined self-care as a radical way to take back autonomy over their own bodies from a health-care system that sought to disregard them.

The Black Panthers in particular enacted much of their

work in the arena of community care and healthcare reform, looking at how poverty and deprivation impacted communities' well-being and what could be done to counteract the negative effects of systemic oppression. Creating free community healthcare clinics, campaigning for community-led housing and fighting for education reform, self-care was a holistic and wide-ranging set of political demands that positioned the practice as not being literally about caring for yourself. Instead, it focused on how we could collectively care for ourselves and each other through an overhaul of institutions riddled with bias and away from the systems that caused harm.

Taking their cues from the Black Panthers, women's liberation activists began running similar campaigns, with both movements creating a self-care system that was equally about survival and utopia. While it was necessary to fight against the rampant racism and sexism that infiltrated every part of life, these programmes were also hopeful. They aspired towards a world in which we all cared for each other. Even online, when I first encountered self-care as a teenager, the posts I read and the people I followed were informing me about aspects of sex education, mental health awareness and bodily knowledge that were completely absent from the classroom or any other form of mainstream discourse.

From the mid twentieth century to Tumblr in the early 2010s, self-care was about respite for marginalised people facing a world with the odds stacked against them. But now, it is positioned as momentary respite from a world in which our injustices feel immovable and impossible to change. We view it as something we use to distract ourselves from feeling shit, rather than a tool that could be utilised to actually pick apart our problems, bring us closer to others and prevent us from burning out in the first place.

When thinking about what self-care means to us now, shopping as respite is transparent enough as a concept that we can see the flaws. But all other forms of popular contemporary self-care also lead back to consumption as central to the practice, no matter how much they veil themselves in good intentions and positive affirmations. The wellness influencers spend huge amounts of cash on their juice cleanses, gym passes and athleisure wear, urging us to do the same through swipe-up links and affiliate discount codes. Meditation apps require monthly subscription fees. The social media personalities who create the quote tiles that inspire us to prioritise ourselves are doing so in order to rack up likes and appease an algorithm that helps supplement their income and raise their profile.

We are not only consuming things that cost us cash, but also eating up every crumb of content that pertains to how others live their lives. We constantly compare our self-care practices to those of others, resentful of those we follow who have more money to spend on tending to themselves and more luxurious routines than ours, and smirking behind the backs of those earnest posters who really do think an inspirational quote will change the world. All of these acts take us away from focusing on ourselves, as we're constantly comparing the way we live our lives with other people who we either feel jealous of or look down on.

In all honesty, most wholesome forms of modern self-care make me nauseous. I'm sick of being patronised by listicles and infographics pulled from basic cognitive behavioural therapy worksheets and reworked by people who would have you believe they invented the idea of self-care themselves. As someone who indulges in the most superficial forms of self-care but also struggles to get out of bed due to debilitating chronic fatigue, I find such lists patronising. The onslaught of well-meaning women posting thirst traps while suggesting we buy a new pair of pants to cure exhaustion is hugely irritating. We are no longer allowed to post a selfie for the sake of a small ego boost or showing off how good we look that day; everything has to carry a meaningful message, no matter how shallow the image.

Self-care has been swallowed up by people with good intentions but zero desire to expand the concept beyond their own individualised problems. Much of my life is spent practising self-care, but in the most boring, tedious and unintentional ways. My illness requires me to be constantly attuned to how I feel, to be acutely aware of my physical and mental health at all times, to know when time out is needed, and to tend to my body's needs in a way that most well people can largely ignore. By and large, the things I have to do to ensure my health doesn't spiral into the territory of Scarily Unwell are not fun.

So, to be constantly met with an onslaught of messaging reminding me to partake in superficial forms of self-care is draining in and of itself. At the very least, visiting the nail shop allows me to forget about my problems for a couple of hours every few weeks. But temporary respite does not make the unfairness of the world disappear. A nice long bath, a lovely scented candle or a two-hour beauty treatment won't solve my problems, but they won't solve anybody else's either. At best, modern self-care is a very expensive way to distract ourselves from bigger issues that seem impossible to face. These methods will always be temporary. As my acrylic nails grow out, my serotonin depletes and the cycle repeats itself for ever more.

We need self-care that does not centre on our individual needs and issues, but instead focuses on pushing against the systems that keep us all perpetually drained and teetering on the edge of nervous breakdowns. In 2021, self-care has mutated into a consumerist catch-all for anything that marginally – and temporarily – increases our ever-dwindling serotonin levels. History proves that the concept of self-care in itself has the potential to benefit communities far beyond those who are dealing with health conditions. However, the commodification of the practice has transformed a once political act into little more than an excuse to buy more stuff.

Ultimately, fighting against these institutions is a protracted and often thankless task. Unlike our current quick-fix self-care culture, results are the opposite of immediate, and long battles have to be fought to see even a marginal amount of progress. Contemporary self-care is unrecognisable from its more radical iterations and the original intended practice of granting freedom to marginalised people. It prioritises individual wants and needs over collective well-being, and forces us all into thinking selfishly and behaving as though our actions do not affect others. This doesn't mean we need to stop treating ourselves. I intend to have my nails done for the rest of my life, take myself for food when I feel shit, and buy things that make me feel good no matter how superficial they seem. But indulging ourselves should sit separately from the school of thought that constantly pushes us to better ourselves by all means possible.

Equally, practising a stereotypically healthy lifestyle of only eating vegetables and hitting the gym five times a week does not make you a good friend, partner, ally or activist. We need to look beyond ourselves – and to look beyond what we think a 'good' person looks like – to see how we can uplift others. We need to aspire to improve the circumstances of our communities, and therefore make our own existences more fulfilling through collective action and care.

If we have any chance of reinstating self-care's meaning and importance, we must pull the practice away from consumerism and back to something that more closely resembles the first instances in which it was applied to social issues. Taking care of ourselves should be practised in tandem with political activism, rather than propping up capitalism. As long as our well-being is pinned on the ability to buy our way out of our negative feelings, our modern iteration of self-care – in my personal experience – is often only similar to slapping a plaster over a gaping bleeding wound.

A love letter to bed

Sleep in the twenty-first century is sold
to us as a luxury. A luxury that has to
be carefully balanced with the demands
of everyday life. One only afforded to
women who have meticulously optimised
their life to allow for it.

My body's relationship with sleep
doesn't feel like a well-wishing friend,
but more of a saboteur.

For most people, a few extra hours spent in bed is one of life's little luxuries. Our beds are our havens. They're often the only place in which we can truly block out the rest of the world's problems. Extravagant brunches on ornate trays can be Instagrammed from a bird's-eye view, with perfectly crisp white sheets. Overpriced, underwhelming face masks can be applied with pride, and luxury pyjamas can be worn as a coded symbol that tells the world: *I am a relaxed human being, I take time to chill.*

Against my will, I've clocked up more hours under my sheets than most people in their twenties – and not in a sexy way. For me, my bed is both my biggest comfort and my worst enemy. My life rotates around it: from work, to sleep, to socialising, to eating, and back to sleep again. While a selfie at home may be a rarity for those who spend their weekends out in the world, I ration the amount I allow myself to be seen on social media from my bed, for fear the mere sight of my covers in the corner of the frame will signal an inability to live normally. My bed is one of the small reminders that as much as I can construct myself as a functioning member of society, often I am not one. While it can be a source of comfort, my place of rest can often feel like a prison.

My co-dependency is not by choice, but because I suffer from chronic fatigue.

Living with debilitating tiredness was not what I expected from the prime years of my life – my twenties. It changed everything about me, from who I went on holiday with, to all the drinks, socialising and opportunities I have had to avoid and the professional obligations I've had to withdraw from. All spontaneity went out the window, and my every move away from the home became dictated by my body's refusal to oblige with my responsibilities.

Chronic fatigue isn't as simple as just needing to sleep. It can't be suppressed by a strong coffee or pushed back with sheer will. My tiredness hits me in the form of joint pains, headaches, brain fog and pain that can't be silenced by anything but a long, deep nap. The reality that I will probably always be tired in one form or another controls many of my waking thoughts and actions. At any given moment, my brain is running through hundreds of tiny calculations, weighing up which tasks I can fit into my day without having to retreat under the sheets, what work I can get done from my bed, and how many hours will be lost to the deep black hole of slumber that I often find myself in. My over-dependence on sleep usually arrives at the worst moments, the periods I've spent weeks revving myself up to in order to ensure they become the most productive yet, when I have deadlines looming, a full social calendar, and commitments that can't be shifted. Simply saying 'I am too tired' feels like a weak excuse. But on the days when my body simply won't comply, it's the only one I have.

As a society, our relationship with sleep has never been more fraught. Each morning, experts on daytime TV advise the nation on how to get more sleep. They tell us that the fact that we're all resting too little is failing us. My sponsored ads on Instagram would have me believe I'm the only person to clock eight solid hours a night and still feel it isn't enough. Animations for meditative apps soar across my screen, offering subscriptions for pillow sprays, soothing games, and ex-boy-band heartthrobs reading bedtime stories, all sold on the promise of helping me achieve peaceful rest.

Insomnia has been found to affect women more commonly than men, with a 40 per cent higher lifetime risk of experiencing problems with sleep if you're a woman, and up to 67 per cent of us reporting that we do. Problems with our sleeping patterns are linked to hormonal changes, stress, depression and anxiety. At a particular point in my life at which my relationship with sleep seemed too fraught to handle, I sought the help of an NHS-prescribed sleep hygiene workshop in an attempt to fix my reliance on rest. Expecting scientific or medical advice on how to help my body fight the urge to slip into slumber, I instead found myself sitting around a table with a dozen other people all sporting the same dark eye-bags as me.

Flicking through pamphlet after pamphlet advising

warm-toned light bulbs, less screen time, and a ban on drinking any liquid after 8 p.m., I felt the weight of my eyelids slowly force my eyes shut, and promptly fell asleep. No amount of handy lifestyle advice can convince my body to start behaving itself. Being told to leave your phone in the living room to avoid distraction when trying to drift off is a handy tip, but it's not one that can be actualised if you're someone who spends most of the day toing and froing between bed, desk and bathroom. While we have found hundreds of excuses to explain why we all sleep too little, the question as to why huge swathes of women suffer with chronic fatigue is largely unanswered. Our symptoms are untreatable, and render our existences an annoying inconvenience to the pressures and pace of modern life.

While oversleeping might be my specific issue, insomnia is a societal one that shapes our attitudes towards rest. Instead of looking at the structural issues contributing to so many people's inability to get a good night's sleep, the world has decided to instead do what it does best: commodify insomnia and sell us back the solution. With so many of us getting so little of it, sleep in the twenty-first century is sold to us as a luxury that has to be carefully balanced with the demands of everyday life. One only afforded to women who have meticulously optimised their lives to allow for it; the ones who wake up and stretch in front of a yoga class, who ensure their bodies and minds are cared for the way society tells us they should be, and who can afford the trendy mattresses peddled to us in podcast adverts. These are the women with five different apps all working to optimise their every moment, a private therapist on speed dial, and enough disposable income to avoid lying awake at night wondering how they'll pay their bills. The ones who aren't chronically ill and can factor in their downtime like clockwork.

Perhaps because of the romanticisation of the time we spend in bed, a common reaction to my overactive sleeping habits is 'your body is telling you to rest'. As if I have been blessed. As if some divine force straight from my subconscious is forcing me to step away from the grind and prioritise myself. It's not that I don't believe in the synergy between our bodies and our minds, that stress can manifest through physical symptoms, or that sleep can be a healing force; it's more that my body is not a friend I have learned to trust. If it really had my best interests at heart, why would it betray me so often?

Being drawn back under the covers feels like conceding to the enemy, my mind and body working against each other. I have no power to stop my eyes slowly drooping, my brain fogging up, and my internal organs rumbling with pain, making me unable to process thoughts. I've seen the sun rise and set countless times without moving more than an inch. I've watched leaves fall and then rebloom from the tops of trees that I can just about squint at from my mattress. Sleep doesn't feel like a well-wishing friend, but more of a saboteur. No matter how much I rationalise that it's my symptoms causing me to be this way, I can't help but brand myself as lazy. The deep guilt that comes with spending so much time 'unwinding' leaves me frequently spiralling, forever perpetuating my abnormal relationship with rest.

Modern life has dictated that a good night's sleep is a privilege, and this is, in part, due to our attitude to work. While we all work overtime and beyond to achieve our dreams, 'burnout' can feel like a pithy word to describe the way in which we've all simply had enough, rather than an appropriate way to signal true exhaustion or suffering. The pressure to succeed early on in our lives means millennial women never clock off; office hours are long, and often followed by hours of side-hustles conceived from home, all laced with the pressure to network with our peers and build our personal brands via social media channels.

To simply do something for the sake of it is unfashionable; enjoyment is out, and monetising our every thought, interest and project is the status quo. Work is often our passion, shaping our social circles, the culture we consume and the lives we lead. Productivity dictates many of our decisions, to the point at which our every move feels like it must be work in one way or another. With the separation between work and our personal lives narrowing, sleep is often the only respite from the pressure to succeed professionally. Although I am still largely prone to falling into this cycle, my condition – the reason for the amount of time I spend in bed – meant that early on in my adult life I had to re-evaluate my relationship with ambition, productivity and work.

Fresh from graduating, I took a full-time staff job at the publication of my dreams. Entering into a notoriously competitive industry, I couldn't believe my luck. For someone who'd grown up watching Blair Waldorf intern at *W Magazine* in *Gossip Girl*, Andy juggling her career and relationships in *The Devil Wears Prada*, and star of *The Hills* Lauren Conrad risking it all for love and deciding not to fly to Paris while interning for *Teen Vogue*, working in the magazine industry felt like everything I had ever dreamed of. Despite the often toxic depictions of these jobs on our TV screens, I was enamoured with the idea of working in a fast-paced environment and climbing the career ladder just as my favourite on-screen personalities had done.

If those pop culture depictions taught me anything, it was that eventually the hard work would be worth it. They showed me that the key to being happy, successful and fabulously dressed is to spend the first ten years of your career working every waking moment, being available 24/7 for your boss's every whim, and sacrificing your personal relationships to get to the top. Landing the role felt like all those hours in university muddling through my first few chronically ill years, pulling all-nighters, taking on work experience placements between hospital stays and building my own publication had paid off. My first stable adult job would help me map out the next twenty years of my life.

My Crohn's disease was in remission, my fatigue stable, and my health concerns felt like nothing more than an occasional annoying itch. Of course, the reality was entirely different. There were no Chanel boots, trips to Europe or long boozy lunches. I was instead put on morning shifts not outlined in the job description, meaning I was having to pitch two news stories before midnight, wake up at 5 a.m. the following morning and file, all before heading into the office and doing a full day's work. While this in itself would mess with any well person's sleep pattern, the post-lunch slump became too much to bear, and I would spend hours fighting the thick fog of tiredness, pleading with myself to push through and make it work.

I was not the only one suffering. The office itself was what can only be described as bleak. We were all on below-average wages, working in an environment with no natural light or windows, crammed desks, and a single toilet built as a sort of shack in the middle of the room – not ideal for someone with irritable bowel disease. No one took lunch breaks, and the anxiety of being judged for what I ate at my desk as a fat person meant I often skipped meals. *But this is what we all signed up for, right?*

We were at the beginning of our careers, cutting our teeth

in the trenches before swanning off to the better-paid and more glamorous jobs waiting for us on the other side. Soon enough, the not-so-silent sobs that could often be heard from the bathroom cubicle would be a distant nightmare for us all. But between unrealistic expectations from senior members of staff, impossible targets and a generally rough working environment, a few months into my dream job both my mental and physical condition began to deteriorate far beyond even my own expectations. It felt like my entire body was screaming at me to get out; I could barely control my bowels, I had daily anxiety attacks, and my stomach would tie itself into knots at the mere sight of my desk.

My work started to suffer. I began to hear whispers from my colleagues that I was falling behind with my articles. One day, I flicked through my web tabs and discovered group chats in which I'd become the focus of office gossip. I saw that my boss had frantically fired off messages to a number of colleagues asking if my illness was even real, wondering whether Crohn's disease was serious and claiming that even if it was, it was surely no excuse for poor performance – they all managed to get by under the same circumstances, after all. Over the course of a few months, I felt more and more frozen out, and more isolated from my work environment than ever before. While the whispers continued, those around me never confronted me, asked me to explain or (in one case at least) even googled my condition. Instead, I was branded lazy.

I finally snapped. My breaking point wasn't the empowered moment of my televised dreams; I didn't berate my boss, throw my phone into an ornate Parisian fountain or ruin an industry party with my rage. Instead I called meetings in which I pleaded with the higher-up members of staff for flexible working conditions, understanding, or even just a simple acknowledgement that what I was experiencing was due to a medical condition. When none of that worked, I quietly quit. On my final day, I slunk away from the office without so much as a goodbye from most of my colleagues, and cried the entire bus ride home.

But at that moment of pure misery, something inside me changed. I realised that while so many of us simply put up with the circumstances we are offered under the illusion of actualising our dreams, pushing through the pain would no longer be an option. With the professional landscape unwilling to accommodate my disability, I had to find another way to live. I am stubborn. Much of my life post-Crohn's diagnosis has been spent convincing myself that I can move through the world and achieve whatever I want to achieve, without the nuisance of my chronic health condition holding me back.

I've worked jobs with dark brain fog that makes it impossible to think, walked through cities on holiday with people who don't understand my condition, as my joints crumble and ache, and forced myself into countless situations that to a well person are part of everyday life but for me are small acts of hostility towards my body that build into a long-term exhaustion that forces me into bed for days on end. Prior to my first big-girl job, I had never been called lazy by anyone but myself. I had worked tirelessly to ensure no one could ever tarnish me with a label that felt like the antithesis of everything I stood for and wanted to be.

Hearing others say it confirmed all the things I feared about myself: that my illness wasn't an excuse, that I was always doomed to fail because of it, and that my career would be curtailed due to my disability. The worst realisation of all was that these were not just things I had thought about myself; everybody else thought them too. Our idea of traditional success is so deeply entwined with suffering that requiring rest is deemed a weakness, or a treat that can only be indulged in once earned.

Leaving the world of traditional work forced me to rewire my brain. I had to embrace laziness. Working from home meant my naps became more frequent, not only as my body recovered, but as I came to realise that I had been punishing myself for living with symptoms far out of my control. The more I withdrew from the nine-to-five grind, the more obvious it became that I would never go back. I've become accustomed to taking the time I need for my body to catch up with my mind. I work when I can, and I sleep when I need to; because even if I resisted the urge to crawl back under the duvet, my usefulness to the outside world would be non-existent. During one of these periods of exhaustion, I can stare blankly at a laptop screen for hours, begging my brain to allow me to start the tasks that I need to complete before the sun sets on the day.

I walk to coffee meetings and post-work drinks feeling as though I've taken a strong sedative, the world warping and slippery. My ill-fated attempt at a full-time job taught me that my bed can't be blamed in and of itself for my tiredness; that comes from inside myself. I can sense sleep peeking over the horizon, with nothing that can be done to stop it – no amount of good planning, healthy habits or medical intervention. It is simply something I have to learn to live with. I still scorn myself for watching another twenty-four hours roll by without leaving my flat for a walk, without getting dressed, or without participating in the hustle culture we've come to expect from my generation.

The guilt sets in like rot as I scroll through my peers cataloguing achievement after achievement while I struggle to find a comfortable position to lie down in. My physical inability to be a get-up-and-go kind of person leaves me feeling as though I'm lagging behind, missing opportunities that should be easy wins and ultimately failing. Being held by the warm covers cannot shield me from the pace of the world. But as I've come to accept that some days it simply won't be possible to drag myself out of the bedroom, I've realised that the negative connotations that come with spending so much time asleep are not ones I've enforced on myself, but rather are a response to the work-obsessed culture we all buy into.

I've had to make my co-dependent relationship with my bed work for me, and in reality, I still achieve as much as anyone who spends their days commuting and working from an office with a rigid schedule. While fear of being perceived as lazy may consume many of my waking moments, the others are spent building a business from between the sheets. I've filed articles, devised magazines, and taken important Zoom calls with the webcam perfectly framing my face so as to hide the duvet encircling my waist. The moments, days and weeks – if I'm lucky – when I can hide from the ever-looming cloud of fatigue have to be seized to their full advantage. My bed isn't simply somewhere I sleep, but somewhere I work from, socialise from, eat from, type from and scheme from. My ability to take to my bed for days on end, unbothered by the world outside of my window, is now a skill I've learned to be proud of.

In the disability and chronic illness communities, a metaphor called the spoon theory has become popular as a catch-all for the type of boomeranging between productivity and extreme stillness that I experience. Coined by Christine Miserandino in 2003 to help her able-bodied friend better understand her limited energy, it goes something like this: two women are sitting at a restaurant table. One asks what it's like to live with chronic illness, and the other pushes the cutlery pot across the table to her. She then asks her friend to list all her tasks for the day: getting up, having a shower, getting dressed, putting on make-up, making breakfast, eating breakfast, and so on. For each task, no matter how small, she has to remove a spoon from the pot, until none are left. The spoons represent the amount of energy it takes to fulfil a task, the limited nature of our energy reserves, and how quickly they are used up. By the time all the spoons are gone, our protagonist hasn't even got out of the front door. This tale is supposed to provide a 'gotcha' moment for well people as they realise that there will never be enough spoons to get through the day.

Chronically ill people all over the world identify with this theory, proudly calling themselves spoonies, using the marker to find other people like them online, and reeling off the story itself as a simple way to explain what goes on in their bodies. I've never really been able to relate to the theory; the link between spoons and the reality of living with limited energy is too abstract for me to wrap my head around, and the idea of proudly identifying as a spoonie seems too quaint. While I understand the desire to make illness palatable and understandable, having to explain the reality that something as simple as going for a catch-up with friends often results in a three-hour nap has never been an experience that I can neatly summarise in a cutesy, endearing way.

Something that takes five minutes to reel off but ultimately means 'I'm too tired to do things' takes up more energy than simply being upfront about my needs without cloaking them in metaphors. The spoon theory feels like an overly nice way to plead for understanding from people who would rather remain wilfully ignorant. I've learned that no matter how real your fatigue is, or how debilitating it feels, no one can fully comprehend that it's impossible to just push through.

We are all tired. We all have days in which we stare at our inboxes, unable to open or reply to a single email. Modern life is exhausting, and we're all overworked. There is a kinship to be found among other disabled and chronically ill people. People who won't mind if you cancel plans shortly before they are meant to begin, who offer you space to nap in their homes, and who you can speak freely with about the amount of time you spend asleep, without fear of judgement.

I've found that understanding of the spoon theory often starts and ends with those who can already relate to it. Instead of using the metaphor as a way to convince others to wrap their heads around the fact that some of us are simply more tired than others, I believe we should all embrace our inner slob. Chronically ill people are forced to re-evaluate our relationship with rest and accept that being lazy is no bad thing, but we could all benefit from easing the pressure we place on ourselves when it comes to productivity. In the end, burning ourselves out works for no one.

I've learned that the urgency we've projected onto modern life is often nothing more than a farce. It makes us feel busy, and that we are doing worthwhile things with our lives, but it also leaves many of us unable to catch a breath. As much as my generation purports to hate capitalism, our entire lives are now structured around it, with our schedules and sleep patterns bending and breaking as we attempt to keep up. Pressure can be good for us, but the expectation for our attention to be on work at all times, and the exhaustion that comes with it, means we're more likely to be fulfilling our obligations at levels far below our capability.

My reliance on my bed should not be a dirty little secret. Those throughout the ages who have embraced their bed as a place integral to their creativity are some of the most revered cultural icons of modern history. Frida Kahlo was bedridden due to her health conditions; Tracey Emin created a masterpiece about her bed that was exhibited at the Tate; Viv Albertine and Joan Didion both wrote bestselling books while propped up by their pillows. These women's ability to create magic from a place of dormancy may have been born from necessity such as illness or heartbreak, but their experiences prove that prioritising rest and remaining productive are not mutually exclusive. Though I often find myself resenting it, my bed allows me space to think. It provides me with the opportunity to really do what I want to do rather than what I feel I have to, keeps my Crohn's disease in relative remission, and helps me focus fully in the moments I can spend being productive.

With much of my time spent asleep, I've learned that my unread emails can stay in my inbox, the world won't crumble if I miss a scheduled Instagram post, and there is no professional task that can't be held off for a few days. Time can, for the most part, be manipulated to work for you. Though I may be napping while the rest of my generation climb upwards in their careers, the hours spent in a dark room can often feel like a fair trade-off when I wake from a long period of brain fog. I bounce back as if months of my life hadn't been lost, and while my pain does not dissipate, my bed becomes a place of productivity rather than confinement. During those periods, my brain runs at a thousand miles per minute, actualising projects, making plans and catching up with all the moments I've missed. After spending nearly the entirety of my adult life so far in this way, I believe we do not have to have an either/or approach when it comes to resting and fulfilling our dreams.

Throughout recent history, our attitudes to achievement and rest have flip-flopped. In the eighties, money ruled, power dressing was king, and in the decade that women's share of corporate management positions doubled, the world became wealth-obsessed. This was quickly reversed in the nineties, when the fatigue of living with rampant capitalism grew and Generation X rejected the status quo in favour of slacker culture, a term defined as perfecting the art of doing as little as possible for as long as possible.

While the eighties prioritised tangible wealth, the nineties pioneered creativity in a way that wasn't tied to commerce. It was a period of youth culture that resented celebrity, celebrated apathy, and glorified the underachiever. Fast forward to the 2020s, and we now live in an era where we are expected to value creativity and achieve financially in equal measure. Millennials and Gen Z are experiencing the worst of both worlds. We must live our lives authentically, yet every move we make needs to add material or social value to our existence, otherwise it is rendered pointless.

Working a normal job to simply pay the bills doesn't cut it, and your hobby isn't worth shit unless you're profiting from it. By blending the material attitude of the eighties with the whimsy of counterculture in the nineties, we have created a monster. Our every move must appear effortless but be financially fruitful. However, if history has taught us anything, it's that another way is possible. Aspiration does not have to only exist on two ends of an equally impossible spectrum. Creativity does not have to be directly linked to our careers, requiring money doesn't mean you're a rampant capitalist, and needing to rest does not make us monsters.

By letting rest back into my life, I had to accept that my achievements might not come as rapidly as those of my peers. That often I would feel like an imposter whose entire life is somehow a fluke, as no one who sleeps as much as me could possibly be successful. But in return, my aspirations have shifted and become much more healthy. By accepting that sleep will always be a massive part of who I am, the reality of our modern, optimisation-obsessed world feels much less difficult to face, and I'm able to carve my own way of living within it.

We could all learn a thing or two from those among us who refuse to compromise on rest, whether their confinement is by necessity or for pleasure. By embracing our beds, we can slowly undo the harmful attitudes that have been instilled in recent generations. My bed allowed me to realise that what I thought I wanted was not in fact my own dream, but ideas gathered up from years of conditioning that taught me the only successful way to live is to work until you die.

Beyond millennial pink

By reducing a political movement
down to the idea that marginalised
people are capable of making their
own empowered choices, the world is
reduced to the idea that we can simply
buy ourselves out of our own inequality.

Being a feminist is an identity we can
slip in and out of at our leisure more
than ever before.

It seems impossible to picture a time in which the daily discourse wasn't saturated with social politics. Throughout the course of my adult life, rarely a day has gone by without an argument breaking out as to what constitutes feminism; whether a particular celebrity is culturally appropriating or appreciating; or if a public figure is correctly checking their privilege. Identity politics and the fight for women's rights are deeply embedded in every corner of our cultural landscape, as well as our interpersonal relationships and workplaces.

Instead of this fairly recent visibility inspiring an entire generation to push en masse for the rights we deserve, we're all exhausted by the faux-empowerment that has been forced upon us. We're so sick of seeing powerful celebrities flexing their feminist credentials that declaring yourself a feminist is more likely to incite an eye roll than facilitate meaningful conversation. The quest for equality has become conflated with everything that is wrong about living in the digital age, with our over-reliance on individual identity politics joining forces with the rise of personal brands to create a movement more intent on chasing clout than changing policy.

Corporations have become the voices of the movement,

pushing equality by emblazoning every sellable item imaginable with a slogan that alludes to girl power and recruiting
influencers to advertise their products under the guise of
empowerment. Away from the corporate world, feminism
feels like a fight to the death of who can perform their
activism the most effectively, rather than striving for the
things that actually cause change. Language once used by
young feminists online is now fodder for bigoted TV hosts
to debate over. Moral panic fabricated by those co-opting
such language has reduced important activist processes
like accountability to dismissive catchphrases such as
'cancel culture'.

Whereas it may now be the case that we can all debate
sociopolitical issues with ease, we haven't always been as
open, nor as well versed in the language and theories that
define our experiences of oppression. Until the tail end of
my teenage years, I wouldn't have been able to reel off a dic-
tionary definition of feminism if you had a gun to my head.
Twitter was in its infancy, Instagram was non-existent, and
my time online was spent customising layouts on Bebo or
lamenting the fact that I hadn't made it into somebody's
top friends list on Myspace. I didn't grow up with access
to feminist texts or surrounded by empowering media, nor
did I have any of the resources available to seek out these
things when I started to suspect that the way we were
existing wasn't quite right.

Had I not one day logged on to the micro-blogging

platform Tumblr, it might have been many more years before I engaged with any feminist arguments at all. Before that, the only real feminist ideas that had etched themselves onto my brain came in the form of watching Mrs Banks stomp around the house wearing a suffragette's uniform in *Mary Poppins*, the Spice Girls screaming girl power, and my mum sitting me down in a very serious manner when I was seven years old and telling me that Vivienne Westwood had invented punk – despite the fact that I had no idea what punk was. The knowledge I lacked and the sense of belonging I craved is now accessible to anyone who's ever glanced at a billboard or opened a magazine.

While there is absolutely nothing to hate about the fact that we can now all access academic feminist ideas that were jealously guarded for so long, we seem to have reached saturation point. We're so used to being bombarded with benign corporate content cloaked in the language of feminism that now nearly everything feels meaningless. In less than a decade, we've come full circle, taking the fight for equal rights from irrelevance into mainstream culture, only to then become so sick of it that we'd prefer feminism to disappear all over again.

Remembering way back to my feminist awakening, it seemed impossible then that as an adult, myself and my peers would distance themselves from the label. Increasingly, a new wave of post-feminism seems like an inevitability. But while we are all fed up of our own politics being commodified and sold back to us, the beginnings of fourth-wave feminism represent a tiny pocket of internet history worth remembering. While we may feel as if we are the only generation to watch the things we care about being turned into marketing fodder, our story is one that has repeated itself time and time again throughout the course of history.

It's easy to blame social media for creating a capitalist Frankenstein's monster mixing politics and commerce, but we aren't the first to use fashion and beauty to fight for equal rights. In the suffragettes' heyday, over one hundred years ago, activists enforced a dress code among their organisation. Concerned with their image and reputation, they encouraged all those engaging in the illegal activities – the ones that eventually won some women the right to vote – to dress in their smartest clothes so as to not be further painted as tyrants or terrorists.

Initially, this tactic was used to distract from their radical politics and covertly gain access to spaces that would allow them to chain themselves to gates, plant bombs and run across racecourses without raising alarm bells. As their battle rattled on, the suffragettes became known for a colour palette of purple, white and green that was seen on both flags and printed matter, but also in their outfits; a uniform emerged that altered their existing dress to mirror their political ideologies. Over time, as the movement progressed, the group began to sell their wares; silk scarves, tops, accessories and even bags named after the suffragettes' most famous figures could be found in shops that worked as part retail experience, part campaign headquarters.

Just like our current iteration of empowerment, the suffrage movement elevated its members to celebrity status and peddled material goods as a form of propaganda. Even if not actively involved in protests, women of the era began incorporating the colours of suffrage into their wardrobes through jewellery or other smaller items of clothing. This is mimicked by the contemporary idea that women can adopt symbols of female empowerment even if they are not fully immersed in the political fight. Selling clothes and using material objects to construct your identity is not insidious in and of itself; many marginalised people use clothes, make-up and hairstyles to assert their place in the world, align with their communities and push back against restrictive standards and stereotypes. In a world that seeks to oppress our existence in so many ways, sometimes the way we look is one of the only things we can fully control.

In the case of the suffragettes, spending power was one of the few autonomous actions they had access to. As department stores such as Selfridges sprang up, prioritising women and operating as places not only to shop but also to congregate without the presence of a guardian, the link between social action and shopping became a natural one, despite being restricted to the middle and upper classes. Selfridges became one of the movement's most high-profile supporters, advertising in the suffragettes' newspaper, which led to widespread support from other stores across London, who would stock 'comfortable' corsets for marching in, dress materials and red lipstick – the latter becoming another symbol synonymous with the movement. The link between fashion and the fight for emancipation became so intertwined that the suffragette newspaper dedicated a whole section of the publication to suppliers and shops that stocked suffragette-related pieces. Despite both the suffragettes and the following second-wave movement being credited for largely focusing on collective action rather than individualist labels, the first inklings of our current movement's aesthetic obsession can be traced back to their beginnings.

But fourth-wave feminism wasn't always synonymous with slogans and self-image. Before empowerment could be found on the back of every razor box, discovering feminism online felt like stumbling upon a secret world that answered all the questions I had about who I was destined to become. I can't remember the first time I heard the word 'feminism', but I do remember what I felt the first time I opened my laptop, logged on to Tumblr and saw streams and streams of pink fill up my homepage. It felt like coming home for the first time; like I'd finally found a place I could truly belong – even if it was in the virtual realm. The now unpopular micro-blogging platform was my way into feminism, queerness and most other forms of social politics.

In its prime, Tumblr, like any social media platform, facilitated different cliques, communities and political positions, many of which have had lasting implications for our culture today, despite the site reaching peak popularity a decade ago. It was a hotbed for fan culture – now stan culture – an incubator for 'wokeness' and 'cancel culture' to be propelled into the popular consciousness, and is labelled by many as the beginning of the end when it comes to pro- ductive sociopolitical discourse. The site fast-tracked our obsession with identity politics, individualism and femver- tising. It didn't incubate one specific school of thought or a singular aesthetic vision, but rather became the go-to place to experience all different kinds of worlds within worlds in the virtual realm.

My experience on the platform was more singular than that of many of my peers. I didn't stray into the realm of fanfiction communities, encounter anime obsessives, or cross paths with the type of twee feminism expressed by Zooey Deschanel's content site *HelloGiggles*, nor the type of discourse that ran parallel with feminist publications such as *The Vagenda* or *Jezebel*. I was largely oblivious to the huge swathes of NSFW content, sad girls stanning Lana Del Rey, and the vast rabbit hole of warped sociopolitics that have come to define the site. Instead, I found my home among visual artists working in the realm of representing and subverting their experiences as femmes.

Although the aforementioned subcultures that made up the labyrinth of Tumblr largely evaded my orbit, they all fed into each other to a certain extent, and shaped the language of sociopolitics in a way that would long outlive the site's popularity. With a large majority – if not all – of these micro-groups geared towards the experiences of marginalised people, it was the first time in which my generation were allowed to curate our own realities away from patriarchal mainstream society. With all the negative lasting social implications Tumblr inflicted on our cultural and political landscape, a lot of good also came out of the site. While those who broke through beyond the platform's realms and became household names were largely white, skinny, able-bodied and cisgender, many marginalised people popular on the platform went on to achieve wide success and become staples of real-life underground cultural scenes.

With many Tumblr users also making zines, publications dealing specifically with the experiences of people of colour such as *gal-dem*, *Diaspora Drama* and OOMK were first conceived from creative communities initially incubated on Tumblr. Lorde, the world's first non-white modelling agency, was also born out of the site. Zarina Muhammad and Gabrielle de la Puente, co-founders of art criticism site The White Pube, found their initial inspiration online and on Tumblr. What made Tumblr great was that it provided a space for the most niche of interests, which caused counter-culture to splinter into different subsections of the internet, despite existing under the same roof. The platform was uncensored, unrestrictive and an incubator for ideas that had often been unheard.

Because of its fragmented nature, each individual's experience on the site was widely different. But once the popularity of the feminism incubated on the site grew beyond Tumblr itself, the small but significant differences of each subsection became eroded, with the sum of its parts compounding into a large, sticky mess ripe for capitalisation. The site reached its peak during a period of time in which life online came without highly curated algorithms. We were free from the tools that now reflect our every thought back at us in the form of suggested content and sponsored advertisements.

Instead, Tumblr was more of a melting pot of ideas from across generations, which could then be boiled down into hyper-specific visual work made by its users. Critical theory sat alongside pastel-pink imagery, which was presented next to Fashion Week images, movie screencaps, diary entries and academic thought. Finding who to follow would take hours of rifling through the interactions of posts you liked and the notes on other users' content. The timeline of the dashboard home feed was chronological, and hashtags were used to write covert notes to followers, rather than being utilised as a tool to boost content. Maybe most crucially, for a long time it was advertisement-free.

Although Tumblr was as much of a popularity contest as any social media platform we use now, no one was monetising their content. Instead, blogs gave young women an opportunity to curate their world view through pop culture moments and sociopolitical thought that could bolster their personal brands or creative work. This pick-and-mix approach to sociopolitics allowed people to construct their own realities, and while it meant that important cultural contexts behind the content found there were often lost, it allowed us to connect with each other based on minute details of our lives rather than overarching structural inequalities. Being obsessed with a particular runway show could lead you to posts exploring the history of that specific societal moment. Falling down a rabbit hole of vintage film stills could result in stumbling into feminist texts about intersectionality. The photography, illustration and creativity of teenagers would be cross-referenced with iconic moments from art history, the two sitting alongside each other as if they were of equal importance.

Because of this, our politics were immediately intertwined with aesthetics. People didn't build followings because of their knowledge of a particular subject, but rather due to their ability to curate an entire online identity that their community related to on a visual, political and personal level. Encountering the collectives, zines and individuals pioneering this visual language was the first time I saw anything close to my reality reflected back at me.

When I think of fourth-wave feminism, I think of one thing: millennial pink. The colour has practically defined my twenties; it has been impossible to ignore, but nor would I ever want to be without it. Described as a warm blush tone, millennial pink holds far more meaning than a quick glance at a colour chart would ever reveal. Reaching peak popularity around 2018, it was catapulted into mainstream consciousness by Drake's 'Hotline Bling' artwork, *The Grand Budapest Hotel* and beauty brand Glossier; it's not an exaggeration to say that it was impossible to blink without seeing a flash of it in every corner of culture at the tail end of the 2010s.

With the rise of fourth-wave feminism, the colour came to represent a new era of femininity, one defined by choice and embracing the perceived flaws of femininity while eroding the gender binary altogether. The aforementioned examples fail to convey just how much of a chokehold millennial pink had on teenage girls and young women in the second half of the decade. A warm tone that had been synonymous with weakness for so long became the perfect embodiment of both everything we loved and all that we loathed. While the obsession with it began as a way for women to reclaim their identity, the colour morphed into the ideal symbol for corporations to wield when choosing to jump on the feminist bandwagon.

Long before the shade could be seen on every billboard, in every music video and shop window, it had been integral to me personally in terms of developing a sense of self. I have always been drawn to pink. As a child, I tried to fight it, intent on the fact that I was not like other girls and was morally superior to those who spent their days fawning over princess dresses and Polly Pockets. Growing up in the early noughties, it was abundantly clear that liking pink meant being girlish, and being a girl meant being less in the world. At the earliest opportunity, probably somewhere between the ages of eight and eleven, I discarded all of my childish feminine trappings and started obsessively pursuing the fact that I was destined to tread a much darker path with regards to personal style, swapping my pink puffy dresses for the goth, pop punk, Avril Lavigne-inspired garb that lined the walls of Tammy Girl.

Growing into my teenage years, my awareness of just how much everybody hated femininity only grew. Anything perceived to be celebrating it was presented as something to belittle, berate or outright mock. Tabloid newspapers tore apart teen pop icons and painted as a bimbo any high-profile woman with a penchant for tiny dogs, bleach-blonde hair and a wardrobe stuffed with shades of pink. Liking these things was seen as not only frivolous, but unintel-ligent; a stereotype that couldn't be unstitched from my brain no matter how many times I watched *Legally Blonde* on repeat. I spent most of my formative teen years pushing any semblance of femininity to the back of my mind and pursuing a 'coolness' that was impossible to achieve.

I spent my weekends watching boys in bands from the back of grubby venues, deliberately ripping my tights and attempting to radiate an aura of being above anything that would make me a 'girlie' girl. I only started to admit my fondness for pink – and femininity itself – as a teenager, in secret, online. What I found on Tumblr as a teenager and young adult was a celebration of the artifice of femininity, with young artists using the then unnamed millennial pink to assert the importance of 'low taste', and the urgent need for inclusivity in our media. Using hyper-femininity as an aesthetic marker to expose the flaws in insidious gendered conditioning and the stereotyping of teenage girls, femmes in my corner of Tumblr created their own visual art movement intent on shining a light on the trials and tribulations of growing up.

With imagery reminiscent of our current pastel-pink tampon adverts on acid, young artists were emboldened by the ease of internet communication, the increased accessibility of photographic tools and the opportunity to find community. Suddenly, work that would previously have been confined to GCSE sketchbooks or locked away in secret diaries could be shown to the world. Focused on personal politics such as body hair and menstruation, and visual references such as My Little Pony and Lisa Frank, the resulting works were both seductive and grotesque; they didn't present femininity as empowering in and of itself, and instead revelled in the grossness of coming of age and all the confusion, rejection and feelings of isolation that accompany it.

These images juxtaposed symbols of femininity with the facets of our bodies we are taught to fear: blood, body hair, fat rolls and acne, with their creators regularly opening up about the darkness within them in lengthy personal text posts chronicling their lives side by side with their artistic work. While these people may have been both inspirational and aspirational to me, the confidence of their artistic vision did not come from experience, knowledge or influence, but rather was the result of pure rage combined with the self-assuredness of teenagers ready to take on the world. These were people who felt as alone and isolated by the framework of femininity and its constraints as I did.

Now, the artists and ideas from which millennial pink was born – the ones who gave me the confidence to embrace myself wholly – feel further away than ever. As today's feminist hellscape forces millennial pink down our throats in the form of decor, feminine hygiene products and slogan T-shirts, it's hard to think of a time when the sickly-sweet shade didn't conjure up thoughts of our current iteration of commercialised female empowerment, in which we're told gender inequality can be solved through individual choices.

It's equally hard to remember a time when pink wasn't prefixed with the term 'millennial', or when our gendered products were merely sold back to us on the premise that we were the weaker sex, as opposed to under the guise of equal rights. But while the use of hyper-feminine aesthetics may incite a knowing smirk, the origins of their popularity felt truly meaningful to me as a sixteen-year-old girl.

The reappropriation of millennial pink exists as part of another movement born from Tumblr-era feminism: the female gaze. Sick of the narrow, restrictive beauty ideals enforced on them through popular media, teenage girls began turning the lens on themselves and their friends in an attempt to create a new visual language, one free of patriarchal restrictions, age-influenced assumptions and over-sexualised depictions of their realities. Bored of an entire visual history constructed by men who painted women as submissive objects, young artists began building a world with female perspectives front and centre. Teenage bedrooms, school bathrooms, corridors and bowling alleys were all captured through the rose-tinted glasses of girl-hood, set among a cast of young women who would have all been deemed too imperfect to grace the pages of any popular magazine.

Mimicking the dreamy gaze of Sofia Coppola, and pioneered by artists such as Petra Collins, an entire generation of femmes picked up their 35mm cameras and started shooting film. Pulling inspiration from a nostalgia for lives they hadn't yet lived and decades that had passed before they were born, these young women used photography to open discussions around identity and perception. Creatives such as Arvida Byström, Maisie Cousins, Rachel Hodgson, Molly Soda and Tavi Gevinson became more prominent on the site, and the influence of the female gaze soared. Every girl in her teens owned a film camera to capture her friends' most personal moments, or ran a style blog in which she fused feminist thought with outfit-of-the-day photos.

These images and idols provided a welcoming cushion compared to the imagery engulfing our lives at the time. Terry Richardson – the now notoriously disgraced photographer famous for his glaring flash, bright white backdrops and sexual assault allegations (which he denies) – was in his prime, shooting barely legal skinny white women in compromising positions for American Apparel billboards that could then be found on every street corner. Richard Kern, an American photographer now in his late sixties, may have taken a softer technical approach to his photography, but his upskirt shots of women who still looked like teenagers had a similar effect on our psyches. Away from the art industry and visual culture, the women in the subcultural spotlight prior to and during Tumblr's golden years were not exactly presented as shining examples of autonomy and independence.

Girls such as Alexa Chung, Cory Kennedy, Sky Ferreira

and Peaches Geldof were the last of their kind, in the sense that they rose to superstardom solely under the watchful eye of the male-gaze-driven mainstream media. Whether splashed across tabloids or shown in glimpses on blogs documenting parties, they rarely had the power to exercise their own voices, and were largely seen as counterparts to brilliant men, often in bands, leaving them doomed to forever exist as muses. Dissatisfied with what we were being offered in terms of role models, young women online, armed with cameras and laptops, chose to rally against a culture that had taught us we should be stared at rather than listened to.

The female gaze, and Tumblr feminism in general, presented an opportunity for someone like me to be romanticised, rather than feeling like I had to aspire to the highly sexualised, waif-like party photos splashed across magazines and my social media feeds. But while the imagery may have felt like something new, I and many of my peers were being heavily influenced by the decades before we were born as we attempted to build a visual language for the future. Taking inspiration from eighties teen films, nineties riot grrrl bands and vintage fashion imagery, artists were romanticising their own existence rather than representing their true, often complicated, reality. They were creating versions of what their idealised life could look like.

Thinking back, it's easy to see that many of the female artists at the time were mirroring depictions of teens throughout the history of popular culture rather than rewriting the playbook altogether. Many of them saw femininity, and being a teen, as a performance, or a type of drag; an opportunity to get dressed up and play out roles in lives they thought they should be living but felt isolated from. Of course, when trying to live an aspirational existence, tropes from the male gaze came into play in their artistic output – with the past century of visual culture being dictated by men, that would be impossible to avoid. Many Tumblr users fell into patriarchal trappings when earnestly attempting to create something that more closely mirrored the authentic thoughts and feelings of an adolescent girl.

But the lived experiences of marginalised teenagers are often miserable and terrifying, and Tumblr allowed us an opportunity to feel alone together. Young female and queer photographers also made significant progress in pushing the envelope beyond pure homage, casting fat people, women of colour, transgender and gender-non-conforming people, non-binary models and disabled people. While the subject matter of early Tumblr feminism seems politically restricted when delving into the vast range of inequalities marginalised people face, it makes sense that creatives not yet into adulthood would focus their fight on looking inwards, and on representation rather than political policy.

We're all selfish as teenagers, obsessed with our own image and how it does or does not fit into the world; and this selfishness was reflected in the narrowness of subject matter in the work created on the site. What seems political to a teenage girl is likely to not be reflective of the fights playing out in the wider world. But through this shared struggle to be represented and taken seriously, Tumblr feminism became something bigger than its individual parts. It developed into not just an aesthetic movement, but an interconnected community with shared values across the world.

By 2011, it had become increasingly obvious that the movement was destined for a bigger audience than a few thousand teenagers spread across the globe, connected by the internet. The vast community on Tumblr eventually birthed Rookie, an online content community for teen girls founded by Tavi Gevinson, and a legitimate space for these young artists to publish their work and find others like them. While Rookie continued to cultivate genuine community, multiple other established magazines started featuring the artists who were big on Tumblr. From there, the wider world started to take notice, and girls barely into their twenties started booking huge advertisement campaigns while sitting front row at the fashion shows they once reblogged from their bedrooms.

Watching Gevinson and other artists rise from our computer screens to become a new generation of It girls was beyond refreshing; these were people who had their own ideas and agendas and wanted to change the world. Fast internet access saw the death of the It girl as we once knew her and the birth of the socially conscious influencer; why would we look for inspiration to magazines that fetishised hierarchical society based on class, body image and beauty when far more thrilling role models existed within our own universes? These were figures who shared intimate details of their lives through their blogs, and felt as close to us as any of our dearest friends.

Their achievements felt more viable than the daughter of a rock star, because if a girl on the internet from the middle of nowhere could do it, there was no reason why I could not. Rookie was a beacon of hope for young women in the misogynist media landscape, and continued to be a truly supportive, collaborative and emancipatory space until its closure in late 2018. For a moment, it felt as though Tumblr feminists could have their cake and eat it too; we could not only create a better world, but also make money while doing so. To watch these people ascend was to watch the world finally take people like me seriously. But in reality, fourth-wave feminism was an apple slowly rotting from the inside out, with none of us realising the direction we were headed in until it was too late.

Tumblr feminism isn't the first of its kind to fall foul of capitalism. The history of women's liberation movements is rife with complicated ties to capitalist culture. Over the past thirty years, the acceleration of the relationship between feminism and commodification has been fast-tracked, but the tug of war between the two is documented throughout modern history. In reality, the pair have always been reluctant bedfellows. Most closely connected to our modern iteration of the fight against gender inequality is third-wave feminism and riot grrrl, a movement that gained traction throughout the nineties and into the early noughties. Early fourth-wave feminism owes much to riot grrrl, with zines such as *Girls Get Busy* taking their visual cues directly from the aesthetic of their predecessor. Bands such as Bikini Kill, Babes in Toyland and Bratmobile led the way, screaming lyrics that addressed rape, sexual abuse, women's safety, class and much more – all while wearing baby-doll dresses and adopting valley-girl accents.

Beyond music, riot grrrl became an entire subcultural movement, embracing DIY culture and meeting in garages to create zines that could be distributed far beyond the towns or cities the riot grrrls resided in. The publications themselves were hand-photocopied, and contained a mix of confessional personal writing, academic articles, collages and even colouring-in pages. Riot grrrl was an all-encompassing culture; one that taught girls they were capable of doing whatever they wanted. It showed young women that their artistic contributions and thoughts were just as valid as those of their male counterparts, and that their rage was not only righteous, but could be funnelled into something productive. On the political side of things, riot grrrl and third-wave feminism ushered in intersectionality, and is often credited as the movement in which identity categories began to splinter into more specific groups. As the experiences of women differ so vastly due to a variety of social and economic factors, these groups began to break away and create their own zines, music and meeting groups.

Much like the waves before it, riot grrrl's heavy hitters are all remembered as white, skinny and middle class. But in reality, the feminists working during riot grrrl encompassed a broad range of issues within their publications pages, from the rights of immigrants to the issue of colourism, how fatphobia should be tackled, and much more. The first inklings of intersectionality can be traced all the way back to the nineties. Although the most marginalised among the riot grrrls may be concealed by the retellings of history, third-wave feminism started us on the path we find ourselves on now. Moving away from purely political methods of activism, riot grrrl cemented the idea that self-expression is an important tool in tackling oppression, no matter what artistic medium you choose.

Though firmly anti-capitalist in its roots, over time riot grrrl became more assimilated with consumer culture. Third-wave feminism was taken up by the mainstream, the Spice Girls started screaming girl power, and riot grrrl eventually imploded. However, its legacy should not be underestimated – riot grrrl fused feminism with popular culture for the first time, and in doing so changed the course of our movement for ever.

During my feminist awakening in the 2010s, I was consuming political theory alongside fashion shows, art and other pop culture artefacts. Chanel was putting slutwalks on its runways, not shaving was the pinnacle of women's liberation, and dying your armpit hair pink was considered a radical act. Embracing feminism as a cultural movement rather than a political one is not inherently bad, but without shared goals and fights, we are doomed to forever be considered cultural fodder, with feminist movements that wash, rinse and repeat the same ideas with few to no societal shifts. Pop culture is an important tool; it can provide mirrors to our experiences, help us find community and allow us to make sense of an unfair world. Assimilation into art, music and mainstream society has allowed the fight for equal rights to be more widely understood beyond academic circles and the upper classes. But modern feminism's proximity to pop culture is also one of the reasons it is so susceptible to commodification by patriarchal structures.

The fact that our role models shifted from party girls to political activists and then back again should have served as an early indicator of the direction fourth-wave feminism was heading towards. The movement evolved beyond a group of artists only recognised by their peers, with the female gaze becoming less about a certain aesthetic haziness or political agenda, and more a catch-all term for any woman operating in creative spaces. The female gaze – through no fault of those who pioneered it – became fodder for corporate feminism, and a way in which to segregate marginalised artists from their cisgender white male peers.

Publications and corporations realised we were pining for representation and began to cotton on to the popularity of young female photographers online. Clickbait article after clickbait article emerged lauding the next big thing in visual art based on gender alone. People still in art school, or even still in high school, were propelled onto public platforms as leaders of their industries. This fast-tracking of careers and practices allowed the artists themselves little room for personal growth; once labelled under the female gaze there was no escaping it. Although the politics of these women progressed, there was no room for them to be fully embraced in the industries that accepted them. Artists felt trapped by the identities they had built from their childhood bedrooms, and pressured to remain in the boxes that would help them gain financial security and social status.

As the cracks in fourth-wave feminism began to appear, popular culture took a sledgehammer to the entire movement. Andy Warhol may have professed that 'in the future, everyone will be world-famous for fifteen minutes', but what he didn't know was that it was more like five; and only if you create a body of work or a personal brand unthreatening enough that it can be embraced and exploited by corporations, magazines and fashion houses. Marketing, alongside our contemporary social media platforms, works on the assumption that if something is a hit, you should perform the same action over and over again.

These young people were forced into that cycle of advertising, but as individual artists, and were urged to create bodies of work on a loop at a period in their development in which they should have been experimenting and opening up to the world. Instead, their experiences became boxed in. Due to popularisation, the complicated personal politics of the imagery began to be washed away when mainstream discussions surrounding the artists emerged. Pastel-perfect pictures were stripped of their sinister undertones, emotionally intricate self-portraits became guides to taking good selfies, and inclusive casting became a tick-box rather than a passion. Through the growing appetite to feature more and more female artists while labelling their work as feminist in and of itself, without interrogating meaning beyond their gender, backwards tropes plucked from the patriarchal photography playbook began to seep through the visual language of the female gaze.

What was once the playfulness of women acting out gender roles became borderline damaging depictions of womanhood that played into the stereotypes marginalised people have suffered under for decades. In order to assimilate with the wider world, moral sacrifices had to be made – and those artists with the most differences from mainstream society were the first to be cut from the picture. Devoid of the subversiveness of existing in the undercurrent, and without the intersectional artists who made Tumblr great, there was little to differentiate most of these images from those found in the pages of the magazines that chose to belittle women as their business model. As commending any and every woman working creatively became the norm, criticism for the patriarchal power structures these people may have been playing into dissipated, and morphed into a cultural moment that prioritised individual choice over collective liberation.

Artists slipped into the background of the movement, making way for influencers who took no issue with pushing damaging depictions of empowerment as long as it sold the clothes that paid their rent. A preference for choice feminism became the norm, and the politics of the female gaze quickly crumbled. By the time Tumblr's popularity dwindled in favour of Instagram, a digital nightmare was playing out in the online realm. Brands caught on to the thirst for content created by women for women, and saw an opportunity to rebrand their tools of oppression as necessities in the fight for empowerment.

Now, it's near impossible to scroll through your feed without running into 'feminist' content that truly only serves to empower the bank balance of whoever posted it, or without finding a brand pushing vaginal health supplements being sold under the premise of fighting the patriarchy. Mimicking the language and political ideologies of early fourth-wave feminism, these brands and individuals more often than not fail to extend their new feminist politics beyond empty slogans and a millennial-pink-soaked campaign. Now, the movement has become as much a part of the patriarchy as everything we rallied against in the first place.

On an individual level, beauty products and fashion can be emancipatory; on a societal level, they represent entire industries that seek to take control over how women look, feel and spend their money. Today we're at a point in which we write off this oppression as emancipatory as long as the individual consumer deems it to be so. 'The personal is political' is the defining slogan of second-wave feminism, a movement that gained traction in the United States in the sixties and had spread across the rest of the Western world by the eighties. With the second iteration of the women's rights movement being born out of other sociopolitical movements such as the civil rights movement and anti-war protest groups, women involved with activism at the time felt sidelined by male-dominated groups and banded together to create their own.

'The personal is political' was born as a clap-back to male activists who berated women for bringing their personal issues – such as abortion, body issues, sex and beauty standards – into radical groups, with the men believing these were problems best combated on an individual level rather than through campaigning. Domestic issues such as household responsibilities and women's rights in the home were also brought into the feminist conversation, with the movement progressing from its focus on legislation towards the ways in which life was unfair for women on a wider societal level beyond the right to vote. The fault was placed squarely on patriarchal society, whether on a governmental or familial level, and the second wave forced pressure firmly on institutions that had the power to change but continued to shut women out.

Feminists questioned why women were expected to stay at home, and challenged the fact that an imbalance of power limited who they could see, how they spent their time, and their autonomy over their own bodies and enjoyment. The second wave also brought feelings into the conversation for the first time; activists argued that the balance of power should not be a fight solely based on reason, but that the way women felt about how society functioned should dictate basic rights. They questioned why women should follow the status quo concerning what they had been told their lives should look like, as opposed to trusting their emotions with regards to what they believed they deserved in terms of quality of their existence.

Through this, they pushed the fight for equal rights beyond a purely political battle. Women began questioning the fairness of their relationship dynamics, their workplaces, and their role in the world. However, they were keenly aware that the conditions they found themselves in could not be shifted through personal, individual choices, and instead sought to dismantle oppression by fighting across different intersections towards common goals. As the second wave dissipated, making way for third-wave feminism, and eventually our current commodified movement for equal rights, the way we interpreted the ideologies born in the sixties movement warped. While 'the personal is political' can still ring true for marginalised people first coming to realise their place in the world, the phrase is now more likely to let individuals off the hook for behaving in dubious ways while acting as a feminist. It allows us to rationalise behavioural and cultural patterns that actively work to enforce our gendered society but individually emancipate those partaking in them.

This misinterpretation can in part be traced back to the shift in how we absorb and participate in feminist activities in the digital age. My introduction to feminist politics was through a desire to learn more about myself, as I'm sure is the case for many, many other teenage girls. Because of that, I found a community of people with shared goals and interests. However, our relationship with how we use the internet has shifted over the past decade.

Where I found a community, young women on Instagram now find influencers. Being a feminist is an identity we can slip in and out of at our leisure more than ever before. Through largely consuming these ideas in online realms, not only is a sense of tangible community and solidarity lost, but it is far, far easier to focus solely on the perception of self than on the oppression of all. The personal is political in the sense that our experiences of gendered violence, inequality, workplace discrimination, healthcare bias and more can all be pinned to personal experiences that alert us to the unfairness of the world as we experience them. But where second-wave feminists used these experiences to band together and form coalitions, our generation use their experiences to promote personal brands that lead to careers, followings and opportunities rather than systemic change.

On a fundamental level, it's not surprising that massive corporations preach female empowerment while failing to secure the rights of their workers on every level of the supply chain and allowing men to flourish at the top of their companies. But on a more micro level, these companies twist and distort the worlds of young femmes, imploring them to aspire to the same corrupt standards but to feel good about themselves while doing it. These campaigns are just as manipulative as the ones that inspired my generation to create work that satirises and reclaims their symbols. By reducing a political movement down to the idea that marginalised people are capable of making their own empowered choices, the widespread oppression of all femmes across beauty, the media and the world is condensed to the idea that we can simply buy ourselves out of our own inequality.

The face of advertising has forever been changed, and while the lion's share of the blame should be placed on those working in these corporations, Instagram feminist influencers are complicit in allowing the world of feminist politics to be forever intertwined with capitalism. The individualist ideologies and influencer-first approach to activism whose seeds were first planted on Tumblr became a business model for a new generation of young femmes determined to build up their individual brands and change the world while doing so. With a pivot to Instagram enabling these influencers to preach platitudes relating to the femme experience with even less context than their predecessors on Tumblr, an aesthetic pioneered by those still in high school has become a catch-all for everything that is wrong with contemporary feminism.

While the fourth-wave feminist movement began by using millennial pink as a shiny veneer that opened up people's worlds to the darker, more nuanced politics of existing in a femme body, the aesthetic is now once again used by corporations and skinny cisgender white women to mask a multitude of sins in the mainstream commodified feminist movement. The fashion and beauty industries historically work on exclusion: if you don't conform, they have a product that'll help you to. While there are valid arguments to be made surrounding the ridiculing of femininity and the misogynist nature of portraying our desire to dress ourselves and wear make-up as frivolous, pairing how we look with our political values and beliefs only seeks to exclude the people who can't partake.

Framing political fights in this way almost guarantees that feminists who most closely align with the patriarchy's view of beauty become the most well documented in the canon of history. In reality, multiple different strands of feminism have run parallel to each other for as long as the movement has existed. Black feminism, fat liberation feminism, Marxist feminism, radical feminism and more are all important components in the fight for equal rights that are often ignored when looking back and reeling off our achievements.

Liberal feminism, beginning with the suffragettes, has always been the movement that we remember and the one that garners the most attention. This can be traced back to its proximity to capitalism, the fact that it maintains other societal prejudices while pushing for certain change and its ease of assimilation to patriarchal society. The newest generation of feminists have never known a world different from the one in which the fight for our rights and the representation of our experiences is tied up with capitalism and our individual relationship to our bodies.

They grew up watching the people they idolise promote products alongside their political views, as if the two have always been interlinked. Through a combination of social media, individualism, capitalism and the perseverance of the patriarchy, empowerment is inseparable from achieving an aspirational social status, basking in wealth and starting your journey with enough privilege to encounter minimal problems along the way. We've reached the point where it's impossible to separate the work of those operating from a point of sincerity from the problematic culture that followed it and that continues to persist today.

At its best, Tumblr-era feminism allowed teenage girls and marginalised young people the first real chance to represent themselves. At its worst, it enabled their fast-developing but still naive ideologies to infiltrate advertising, the media and our society at large in a way that has distorted feminist politics as we know it. Our culture has always been obsessed with youth, with the fashion industry and media world fetishising age as a marker for our beauty, relevance and value to society. But more often than not, teenagers have always felt left out of the equation when it comes to any real decision-making. Adolescence is a time in which our world is at its most confusing; we're angry and alone and don't necessarily have all the tools to piece together our thoughts and feelings.

But with access to the internet, a group of femmes in their teens found a way to work out these frustrations through creativity, blogging and learning from each other. Looking back, what none of us realised was that our perspectives on the world would be catapulted onto the global stage; whether overtly through celebrity status, or covertly through artistic influence across visual culture. With our ideologies still developing, and a disproportionate amount of power being handed over to those with no idea how to effectively wield it, what began in earnest became a monster. The work was never intended to make its way back to the origin of our unhappiness: advertising.

Marketing as an industry has always been desperate to sell as much as it can to teenagers and young adults, but has forever struggled to understand them. Through Tumblr, we unknowingly handed the people with power the keys to our minds and welcomed them in. Fourth-wave feminism was conceptualised by a generation that had been bombarded by gendered messaging more than any other. From our TV and computer screens to billboards, magazines, toyshop aisles and runways, we soaked up every message that told us we should be skinny, shaved and submissive.

The visual expression of Tumblr feminism was our way of spitting it back out; of rejecting everything we had been told about womanhood and building our own femme fantasies. What we didn't realise was that our every move was being closely monitored by the patriarchy. That in a few short years, the thought of millennial pink would ignite a knowing smirk or eye roll from a generation disenfranchised by their politics being used to peddle products. The reclamation of these symbols was not intended to normalise their aesthetic use in the wider world, but rather to expose the dangers of revealing these ideas to an entire generation of young people. In the commodification of fourth-wave feminism and its corresponding visual world, young women were momentarily afforded their flowers and allowed to thrive. But in the long term, we are back exactly where we started.

When considering the legacy of Tumblr feminism, it becomes obvious that the movement was always doomed to be commodified, as so many of its predecessors were. Millennial pink became the colour of the decade, private women's members' clubs opened and crumbled, and we're now all feeling exhausted by the pressure to constantly feel empowered. This ongoing tug of war between mainstream and underground recognition for feminist ideals signals an end to the purity and political nature of feminism in each cycle. As this pattern repeats itself over and over, the same question remains: is a diluted movement better than no movement at all?

In previous iterations, the answer is maybe yes. Accessing feminist texts used to be restricted by institutional gate-keeping, racism and classism. But from riot grrrl right up to Instagram, the way we consume culture has changed. Anyone likely to step into a high street store and purchase a girl-power T-shirt has the opportunity to unlock an entire world of female empowerment through their phone screen. Equally, the pressures of the patriarchy are more prevalent than before, and modern feminism feels more hopeless than ever. Not only does a male-dominated take on the female gaze infiltrate the shops we frequent, the bars we visit and the institutions we work in, its power can also be found in our phone screens.

The agents of the modern patriarchy are covert. While the internet once felt like a freeing place, marginalised people are now censored on social media platforms within an inch of their lives. Far-right groups use the same tools that were once developed by feminists, twisting educational infographics to indoctrinate people to their cause. Scrolling through our feeds, it's impossible to differentiate between what's made by a company, created by an individual or conjured up by even more sinister evils that hope to shatter the fabric of radical, left-leaning social politics for ever more. On an individual level, we exist as commodities in an extremely acute way, with our online footprint being sold as valuable data to men who can control the world we live in.

When I feel hopeless, I can't help but succumb to nostalgia and burrow down a wormhole of Tumblr feminism's glory days, remembering the euphoria of feeling on the precipice of something that could truly change the world. While it seems as though our feminist politics have been lost to capitalism, history proves this is not the case. As quickly as faux-empowerment has been accepted into the fold of everyday life, it can be removed, allowing us an opportunity to reinvent feminism for the umpteenth time in our history.

Wallowing in what might have been won't change the fate of the fourth wave, but tracing our mistakes to ensure they are not repeated may well help us do better moving forward into the future. Feminism, in my opinion, should never be disregarded, no matter how enraging it is to see the fight for equality become synonymous with everything it stands to destroy. But it is only through perseverance, and not dismissal, that we have any hope of pulling the movement from the rubble and into the next stage of its existence.

Coping mechanisms

For all the times we rely on seemingly meaningless coping mechanisms to survive the shittiness of life, there is someone waiting in the wings to exploit our insecurities and capitalise on the things that make us feel better.

Where we used to sit around tables with our friends, drinking too much wine and screaming into the void like banshees, we now search for meaning online.

We all diverge in the ways we avoid, and cope with, the omnipresence in our lives that is the void. We fill our days with meaningless tasks, working ourselves to the point of burnout, to ignore the diminishing state of the wider world. We spend our free time cramming as much social interaction into our evenings and weekends as humanly possible. When we're not with our friends, we spend hours scrolling our social media feeds to feel closer to people we either know intimately or have never even met. All of our coping mechanisms are different – but ultimately, we're all searching for the same thing: meaning. Or at least a way to suppress the lack of it that would otherwise consume our lives.

Our coping mechanisms tend to defy logic. Most of us are aware that what comforts us in the short term does not necessarily aid our growth in the long run; like the girl who holds us while we cry in the toilet cubicle of a club after one too many drinks, their ability to soothe us is fleeting. From drinking, smoking and late-night karaoke to binge-watching Netflix and eating Greggs multiple times a week, not all of our coping mechanisms are healthy. But that doesn't automatically render them unhelpful. Ordering takeaway has saved my life more times than I can count, as has FaceTiming a friend and putting the world to rights. Coping mechanisms, ultimately, are there to help us forget the feeling of being entirely alone or without purpose. But these small acts are no longer personal quirks that we utilise at the point we need them. Escaping the void is a generational plight, and one we've come to understand as just another thing we can fix as opposed to coming to accept.

For all the times we rely on seemingly meaningless coping mechanisms to survive the shittiness of life, there is someone waiting in the wings to exploit our insecurities and capitalise on the things that make us feel better. While our personal coping mechanisms can be dismissed as ridiculous but effective, and unworthy of intense scrutiny, in recent years a new, more troubling form of self-help has cropped up alongside the rise of social media. Where we used to sit around a table with our friends, drinking too much wine and screaming into the void like banshees, we now search for meaning online.

Open Instagram, TikTok or any other app of your choice, and you'll likely be met with a slew of stories and posts advising you on small tips to help you live your life in a more positive way. These accounts and influencers promise the one thing that many of us have never quite been able to effectively grasp: being totally and unapologetically at peace with ourselves. Now, instead of buying a self-help guru's book or attending their tour, we have handy infographics constantly available at the click of a finger, force-feeding us all we could ever want to know when it comes to living our lives in the best way possible and avoiding the void by all means necessary.

Even for the most stringent of cynics, those who have come to accept the void as an old friend, digesting these influencers' thoughts isn't optional. If you aren't following these people who consistently ram pseudo-psychology into our brains, then your friends are reposting them on their own profiles, or they are lurking in your 'explore' and 'for you' pages, waiting patiently to strike and indoctrinate you. All it takes is to click on one post for your suggested content to unleash a sea of aesthetically pleasing text. Ranging from the mostly innocuous – 'It's not a dumb idea, your dream is achievable', illustrated with a line drawing of a VW camper van – to the slightly more pointed 'Sending love to everybody who's trying their best to heal from things they never discuss', and the absolutely inappropriate 'Five ways to break your trauma bond with a narcissist'.

The more you click, the more these posts shift from slightly silly 'I'm proud of you' sentiments to information that will have you diagnose half of your friendship group with a personality disorder and become convinced you should totally isolate yourself from everybody around you. Whatever the issue, self-defined thinkfluencers are on hand to advise you on every facet of your existence: from how to cut off toxic friendships and value your own worth, to how your astrological alignment affects your mood and which charitable donations are most pressing. These easily digestible quotes and snippets of insight represent the changing face of our coping mechanisms, introducing my generation to old-school self-help under the guise of new-age empowered thinking.

But they also affect how we talk to each other, shifting where we seek emotional support: from those around us to strangers online. These influencers feed the problem while also promising the cure; we're all so desperate to optimise our circumstances that we're willing to be sucked in by ideas that are actually more likely to damage us. Advice that would probably be considered outdated and cringe-worthy if it was spoken by a man in the eighties wearing a boxy suit and promising that you can win at life is now accepted as important life lessons when filtered through a skinny, white, beautiful spokesperson with a hefty social media following. Despite the fact that social media itself has become a breeding ground for pseudo-psychology and misguided self-help, we've managed to repackage these ideologies as not just good for the individual, but sociopolitical exercises.

All of this information is presented in the same way: a nice font, a brightly coloured background, sometimes an aesthetically pleasing illustration sitting alongside. The range of subjects makes us believe the personal is political; we consume a 'dump him' post alongside slides outlining injustices, placed next to quippy anecdotes on how anyone who purports to hate you is really just 'intellectualising their jealousy'. This leads us to consider each subject with the same weight. Realising that men are trash becomes as important as unpicking racial injustice. Accepting that chronically ill people are real is followed by words urging us to not accept difficult people in any form. The sentiments contradict each other over and over again, but are so personally pointed that we soak up every word, convinced that we'll wind up less alone and a better human being because of them.

Being unwell, it's easy to be sucked in by these people's ideas. If you are someone who spends much of their time feeling like shit for reasons that cannot be explained or cured medically, opening your phone and being met with a whole host of people who claim they understand you and can help improve your life is a comforting idea. But chronically ill people are not the only ones who find it difficult to resist the charm of a pseudo-political platitude. If you're arguing with a friend, there's a thinkfluencer on hand to tell you that cutting people out is the most empowering thing you can do. For a period of time as I neared my mid twenties, my life felt consumed by the advice these individuals were dishing out.

I was spending my time with people I didn't like very much, constantly engulfed in drama largely of my own making, and desperate for any way out of the mess I had found myself in. I started cutting out 'toxic' people left, right and centre, feeling so out of control of my actual life that I would take any actions necessary to regain the feeling of being more myself. I wasn't following any of these social media gurus, but their language had infiltrated my actual real-life interactions so deeply that it felt like their posts were constantly playing on a loop in my brain. I would share their work to my private Instagram account – in an obvious bid for attention – as if I was making empowered decisions, while romanticising the fact that I was setting much of my personal life aflame.

Dig beneath the surface, and these influencers' ideologies are at best flimsy and at worst damaging. They operate in the knowledge that we are all conflict-averse but constantly seeking affirmation. It's much easier to relate to one of these people's posts and remove the people you are having trouble with from your circle entirely, rather than trying to work through any problems you have with friends you probably do in fact deeply care about. We want to constantly feel supported, with these accounts promising to provide us with the tools to live in a more emotionally aware way.

Really, they convince us to put our feelings first and disregard anyone else who dares to challenge us. While of course it's not the job of those with social media accounts to cure mental illness or soothe those living with long-term conditions, these influencers claim to arm you with a toolkit to improve your life, when in actuality, their advice seeks only to line their own pockets by capitalising on other people's insecurity and pain. By isolating their audiences from people who would be lovingly critical, they create parasocial, co-dependent relationships with their followings that keep people coming back for more reassurance that their actions are not shitty, but necessary to self-preservation.

These new-age thinkfluencers are the latest in a long line of people we have turned to in the hope of easing the burden of everyday life through search for meaning. As demonstrated by the eternal draw of psychics, mystics and astrologers, humans are far more likely to seek comfort and support from those who can affirm our feelings than from the facts that cause us to question them. Throughout history, women and marginalised people have been particularly drawn to guidance that veers into the spiritual when seeking comfort in dire circumstances. With many of us relying on non-traditional familial structures or communities, the looming fear of loneliness is always lurking just around the corner. Our search for meaning also feels more fraught, with the likelihood of rejection that leaves us questioning why we are who we are.

It's never been easier to find content that not only soothes us, but convinces us that its creator is someone who can genuinely solve all of our problems. We are literally less than three taps away from discovering a new coping mechanism at any given moment. Yet at the same time, the online world makes us feel utterly helpless. On the one hand, we spend so much of our time scrolling that we truly can't all hate social media as much as we claim to. It's impossible to claw my phone away from my hand. I love ridiculous TikToks of cats falling over, I love the artists I discover through these apps, and I love the friendships I continue to foster on these platforms. However, it's obvious that we've all absolutely had enough of living our lives around phone screens. We spend countless hours telling our friends how paranoid, insecure and hopeless Instagram makes us feel. We delete apps for hours, days or weeks before meekly crawling back after realising that modern life is practically impossible without them. We follow people who make us feel rubbish, idolise celebrities we will never meet, and accept being censored within an inch of our lives. The problem is, when trying to avoid the shittiness of online life, we often fall into the same content traps that made us feel so helpless in the first place.

We believe these infographics are paving the way for more honesty, integrity and vulnerability in our online world. We also want the people we follow to self-correct when their behaviour feels off, just as we rely on them to make us feel better while simultaneously making us absolutely hate ourselves. In reality, we're not tackling the void by taking the advice of someone on the internet that we find aspirational or interesting. All we are doing is consuming the same shiny veneer of authenticity and meaning that we have all grown sick of, but in different packaging. The bad parts of the internet feel impossible to escape from, meaning we cling on to any small semblance of hope, even if it does arrive in the form of an entirely meaningless infographic. We're so desperate for answers that we cling to accounts that feel like the people we love the most, and follow their musings as if they are gospel.

While constantly scrolling in an attempt to escape the void, my generation has found yet another way to fight off the fear that everything is pointless: spiritualism. These think-fluencers may seem at odds with methods that convince us there is a higher power, but the opposite is true. We look to these people as millennial spiritual guides, who fuse the practical with the unexplained to create a toxic cocktail of tools to optimise our consciousness. When used alone, online, self-help Instagram accounts may be read as shallow. But being clued up on which spells help ground you, how to charge your crystals and what the symbols of nature mean signifies to the world that you are above the superficial world of social media.

While the two worlds seem entirely separate, the rise of mystical thinking would not have been possible if not for the facilitation of these practices in online spaces. Huge swathes of the internet are dedicated to spiritualism, and it no longer exists in its own niche corner. Entire apps are dedicated to cross-checking our astrological compatibility with friends, family and potential romantic partners. How-to guides teaching us the importance of setting up salt lines in our homes to protect us from bad energy sit seamlessly alongside outfits of the day and tutorials on how to perfect winged eyeliner.

Astrology, tarot cards, moon cycles, crystals, burning sage and other witchy rituals have become second nature to millennial women. We've accepted these practices into the folds of our lives as if they are as natural as brushing our teeth each morning. I wouldn't consider myself a spiritual person, and I'm definitely not religious. But to a certain degree, my introduction to these ideas came long before our current obsession with all things other-worldly. I grew up immersed in new-age spirituality. My grandmother was obsessed, buying me a deck of angel cards for my birthday, showing me photos of her aura, and slipping a rose quartz into my pocket at every opportunity. I remember hushed conversations as my mum tried to talk her out of attending groups that involved seance rituals in order to commune with the dead.

But even my mother bought into this thinking to a certain degree. My name, Ione, means amethyst in Greek – which is also my birthstone. While pregnant and on holiday in Corfu, she found a lump of it on the side of the road, and decided then and there that it would be my name. I remember huge chunks of the stone all over the house growing up. It was fate. Well, fate and the fact that actress Ione Skye was doing the promotional rounds for a new film that summer. I always thought of my family's adjacency to these beliefs in the same way I thought of fairies, mermaids and witches. Fun, and nice to believe in, but something you should never take too seriously or build a life around.

There was always magic in my childhood home; we believed our house to be haunted. I truly thought Father Christmas was real until I was twelve, and I used to write notes to fairies and leave them in the garden – to which I would receive replies in the form of tiny handwritten letters that were definitely painstakingly penned by my mum. The way I observed spirituality growing up was as a shallow escape, and a series of meaningless rituals that detached you from the mundanity of normal life. These objects and ideas always bubbled away in the background, but never really seemed like a fundamental belief that had to be taken seriously.

My introduction was separate but not removed from a city-wide obsession with spirituality where I grew up in Brighton. My friends and I came to refer to this specific stereotype as 'crusties'; they would always be white, always middle class, always have dreadlocks, and always be appropriating somebody else's culture. You could find them surrounding the grounds of the Royal Pavilion, or on the beach, hitting some sort of bongo drum, smoking weed, sitting on a blanket they'd procured from a life-changing trip to Asia and waxing lyrical about how the world is run by the Illuminati.

Honestly, these people were the final nail in the coffin when it came to my cynicism towards spirituality. North Laine, an independent shopping district, was at that time littered with shops run by ageing hippies selling incense, clothing made of hemp, and books instructing the reader on how to correctly align their chakras. It was impossible to escape from, and I found it all unbearably cringe-inducing. While my friends went to festivals, wore harem pants and had life-altering experiences taking shrooms, I withdrew from all forms of spirituality. That is, until I got Instagram.

In the same way that a specific type of pseudo-spirituality has gripped my entire generation, I too am not immune to the allure of looking to the universe for affirmation, though believing that there are other forces at play regarding my destiny is more depressing than liberating. It would be convenient to berate the gods, or Mother Nature, or even the solar system itself for lumping me with chronic illness, but doing that would also suggest to a certain degree that I deserve to be ill. It's more comforting for me to go through life feeling as though everything is horribly coincidental, and deal with the cards that I've been dealt as they come, rather than believe my entire trajectory has been mapped out by an elusive spiritual force that holds my well-being in its hands.

I also can't afford to allow the universe to hold my destiny in its hands. Counting on spiritual methods to control my symptoms and emotions would literally be like playing Russian roulette with my life. Most of the time, how I spend my days looks like the exact vision Gwyneth Paltrow's Goop advocates against. My existence is completely dictated by science. My fuel of choice is medication that alters my insides to ensure they don't kill me, rather than a blend of herbal teas that promises to keep me zen and attract good vibes. It's hard to see the power in a force bigger than all of us when you spend so much time under the cold light of waiting rooms instead of frolicking in fields during the summer solstice.

When I'm attempting to feel spiritually aligned as opposed to medically well, I mostly gravitate towards ultra-meaningless coping mechanisms. I'm far more likely to turn to a stupid pop song or my favourite food than a deck of cards that promise to predict my future. Honestly, I would rather seek affirmation and comfort than enlightenment or the opportunity to find myself by looking inwards. I understand that meditation supposedly provides a longer-lasting peace than eating a packet of crisps. But whenever I've tried to centre myself on a spiritual level, or zone out the world and align my body with nature, I can't help remembering all the rotting parts that exist beneath my skin.

Saying that, I still hold a candle for the type of astrology and spirituality that has lurked in the background my whole life. I'm the type of person who hates being told that the moon is affecting my mood; I find it reductive, patronising and ridiculous. At the same time, I love to blame every single one of my problems on Mercury retrograde. I know everything about my own star sign and have studied the horoscopes of all my friends (and enemies). I can tell you with full confidence that Geminis are the devil, every journalist I know is a Libra, Capricorns are sweet angels, and my placements of Aquarius sun, Leo rising and Scorpio moon make me an absolute nightmare in most people's eyes.

While spirituality is presented to us as one of the tools we can use to optimise our lives, make ourselves more grounded, deepen our psyche and reconnect with nature in a meaningful way, the reason I manage to find joy in it is not because it makes me feel like a better human. In the same way my grandma used her spiritual gifts to show me she cared, spending two hours talking about astrology feels like a coded language femmes can use to deepen their connection to each other. I don't expect tarot cards to change my life, but reading them with friends is a shortcut to discussing deeper feelings that may have not been unearthed otherwise.

Spirituality, to me, is closer to intimacy than it is to the gods. I grew up watching *Sabrina the Teenage Witch* and *The Craft*, in which spells are associated with female kinship, not self-progression. The internet has allowed girls like me who dreamed of joining a coven growing up to bond over scented spell candles regardless of their actual effectiveness. For someone who forced all their friends at a sleepover to recite 'light as a feather, stiff as a board' on the off chance one of us would begin to float, indulging in astrology and witchcraft is a way to fast-track friendships, and not necessarily a desperate bid to alter reality.

The link between social media and spirituality may be much maligned by diehard mystics and serious witches. There is also no reason to fully trust the credentials of all the people behind these astrology apps and Instagram accounts – with one of the most popular admitting to trolling their users with negative predictions to better prepare them for future bad periods in their lives. Trusting not only this tech, but spirituality in general, to be the guiding force on which you base your decisions will most likely lead to unhappiness in the long run.

Our obsession with these tools may have led to high street stores selling spell kits, and bookings at retreats that promise 'digital detoxes' skyrocketing. But all these negatives do not have to cancel out the connections that can be made through a shared love of the unexplained. I will probably never stop sharing the Powerpuff Girl screenshot that correlates to my sun, moon and rising sign; but I also understand that blindly following the advice of Insta-astrologists will not necessarily improve my life. Our desire to embrace the unknown and our addiction to the internet do not have to exist at odds with one another.

*

Our relationship to social media is fraught in the first place as we're all desperate to find like-minded people but are instead bombarded with aspiration and hierarchy. We're searching for connection – whether platonic, creative or romantic – and the early years of online living hinted at a utopian future in which this was possible. The people who found vital friends in their teenage years on the internet were suddenly lumbered with the expectation of converting those friends, followings and profiles into something more tangible, and ultimately profitable. We saw the internet as a way to be more authentic; to show the parts of ourselves that we were not ready to show the 'real' world. But over time, these communities were replaced with audiences, and personal text posts were swapped out for captions laced with toxic positivity and dubious therapeutic advice.

Now, we are constantly consuming the illusion of authenticity and accepting it as the real thing. The conversations that are usually reserved for the queue for the girls' toilet and drunken rants with your best friends are now posted as gospel not only by individuals, but by brands and influencers with millions of followers. These moments of hyping each other up are affirming when they occur in the real world. We've all revelled in the times our friends pick us up after a nasty break-up or friendship split, screaming about how the other person involved is shit in a desperate attempt to regain a fraction of our self-worth. But while we treasure the words spoken by people we trust or uttered by those we find fleeting connections with in a tipsy haze, constantly consuming these thoughts via our phones does not cultivate the critical thinking that often follows these euphoric moments.

No matter how much we love our friends, we know that their advice cannot always be followed to the letter. We see their mistakes, their moments of stupidity, and we watch them trip up over all of the same issues we encounter ourselves. While there is no pleasure in watching the people you love stumble, it does allow us to contextualise the ways in which they build us up and how they suggest we live our lives. The difference between these chats and their online counterpart is that we don't believe our mates' drunken rambles to be the authority on any given situation. Even though we are all aware that the internet is a Petri dish of misinformation, we're likely to trust whatever pops up in our own curated feed as truth.

We believe in the benevolence of those we follow; why wouldn't we? What would be the point of spending hours creating a pretty graphic if the points it made weren't actually true? We are constantly being told, via the form of infographics, that we are 'enough', that we deserve to follow our dreams, and that individual happiness should be valued above all else. These messages are phrased as if the poster is staring straight into our soul. We trust the accounts we follow with our most fragile of feelings, even if we have never had a personal interaction with them. But these platitudes are as void of meaning as the 'live, laugh, love' signs that hang in our parents' houses. Yes, they are nice sentiments, but in actuality they mean very little.

As we rely on these accounts to bolster our self-esteem, we slowly retreat from seeking it from the people who exist outside of our phones. While we are all desperate to become the best versions of ourselves, research has found that this swing towards individualism actually depoliticises society, and that high self-esteem does not lead to an upwards trajectory of success. Still, we believe these people hold the secrets to a happy, more empowered existence laced with self-confidence. Their lives seem great; they build careers off the back of pithy quotes, have nice clothes, great friends and flawless beauty regimes. Often, buying into these people's ideas is the easiest way to replicate them. Their sponsored posts may contain beautiful dresses, but the majority of us cannot afford to become carbon copies of our internet faves. What we can do, however, is follow their advice and hope some of the stardust that engulfs them rubs off on us.

My days of idolising thinkfluencers are long behind me, but so many of us are understandably still bewitched by their charms. Moreover, their advice may go beyond innocuous lifestyle changes to perpetuate genuinely harmful coping mechanisms. Whether our drug of choice is wishing on a star, or double-tapping on an inspirational quote, one thing is for sure: our lives feel more out of control than ever.

There is comfort to be found in building one's day around the instruction of an astrology app, choosing who to date based on their star sign or shooting down personal problems as the fault of the moon. Similarly, thinkfluencers provide a guiding light of personal politics, leading us through a chaotic life via unqualified therapeutic techniques, ethical consumption and personal optimisation.

When our emotions feel too dark to face, we can just open our phones and be comforted by the words of some-body who seems to have it much better than we do. Both of these modern forms of coping mechanisms have our generation in a chokehold. It seems unlikely that we'll ever wade out of our love–hate relationship with the online world, but one thing we can do is hope for better, while doing whatever it takes to muddle through. I will never begrudge someone finding solace in the words of a stranger, or turning to tarot religiously. But we do need to accept the wider implications of putting feelings before truths. That sometimes, despite how often a decorative text post may tell you otherwise, you are not the centre of the universe, or immune from making mistakes and behaving like a bad person.

Instead of berating ourselves further, we need to ques-tion those who constantly assert that the only way to cope is to centre yourself. Their motives may seem pure, but ultimately, self-help is once again big business. When dubious sources of comfort become gospel, our reliance on them creates more problems than it solves. As long as we are hurting, thinkfluencers continue to rake in cash, creating a cycle of pain and self-pity that it does not make economic sense for them to solve, no matter how hard they try to convince us otherwise.

Inside all of us is a gross girl

We have no framework for where our rage can go, what it can do, or the implications of unleashing it.

Only through accepting the full nastiness of our world, and our own complicity within it, can we move forward progressively towards a more equal society.

In more ways than one, the first part of my life has felt like a horror film. I haven't spent these years being chased around town by serial killers in masks, haunted by ghosts in my bedroom or watching on as my friends murder our classmates with reckless abandon. But as my health declined, I became less and less in control of my own body. I couldn't predict whether a juice drink would cause me to vomit uncontrollably for hours on end, or if the churning pain in my stomach would stop me dead in my tracks halfway down the street. A feeling similar to the moment just before an on-screen jump scare would course through my veins, a bodily instinct that warns us to be scared of what will happen next, the moment I could feel the onset of a flare-up.

My rotting insides were becoming impossible to hide, as my skin morphed into a grim shade of grey, I could barely walk without twisting an ankle, and my eyes were set in hollows of deep blue that told the world just how sleep-deprived I really was. As I came to more closely resemble a corpse bride than a woman blooming into adulthood, I slowly realised that I was becoming the thing that I had always feared: I was a gross girl.

We've all been horrified by our own bodies at various

points in our lives. My own personal realisation of just how disgusting our physical forms really are came from my diagnosis with Crohn's disease, but deep down I knew long before my body started malfunctioning that being prim and proper was never part of my destiny. I would argue that a gross, horrible girl lives inside all of us. We all downplay the satisfaction of squeezing a huge spot, pretending that the pop of a yellow head absolutely repulses us. We pretend to have never skipped a shower, and that our hair definitely hasn't been greasy for the second day in a row. We all profess to have absolutely never picked our noses or pulled at a scab just for the hell of it. But for me, my own disgusting body became impossible to ignore. I was condemned to spending my life consumed by a fear of never achieving acceptability, leaving me with no other choice than to embrace the fact that gross girls not only have more fun, they're the ones that get shit done.

Horror films are as much of a teenage rite of passage as puberty itself. As our bodies rebel, so do we; our first experience of sneaking into the cinema underage – or, now, streaming a slasher film on Netflix – often coincides with the confusing sense of horror and accomplishment of our first menstruation. As a teenager, I would spend hours at the weekend sifting through charity-shop VHS bargain bins. I didn't grow up pre-DVD – I am firmly a product of the internet age – so my reasoning for seeking out this now-ancient tech wasn't necessity or nostalgia. But despite the fact that I could just as easily have streamed any film I could think of, I would lug home carrier bags full to the brim with 99p finds and plug them into the TV/VHS combo player that was a relic from my childhood. Just as finding that one amazing vintage dress for less than a tenner in a bargain bin floods our bodies with serotonin, I felt the same thrill when pressing play on a video tape resulted in discovering a film that would change my life.

Reliant on my completely uncurated treasures, the films I bought would vary in genre and decade. But I quickly found my niche in horror films, and more specifically, the corner of the genre that showed me that femininity wasn't all good wardrobe choices and sleepover clubs. I began to seek out tales not just of rebellious teens bucking the will of their parents, but of young women who transformed into full-on evil horror heroines. As my body began to change with adolescence, my filter on the world shifted. Experiencing all the emotions of a stereotypical teen – rejected, self-conscious and finding it hard to fit in – I found the sanitised version of womanhood I saw in the pages of magazines and on screen trite, and horror films felt like my home.

But despite the kinship I found with horror heroines growing up, it would be hard to imagine just how relevant these depictions of bodily rebellion would become to my adult life. These on-screen horror transformations that occupied hours of my adolescence, particularly when doubled with physical change, came to hold up the perfect mirror for my experiences of being diagnosed and living with chronic illness. While we all like to pretend that the gross parts of ourselves are non-existent, the disgusting things that only rear their head rarely in the case of most people's bodies are a regular occurrence for me. But well or unwell, the horror genre has no regard for the things we try to hide, and instead lays bare the parts of ourselves we'd all prefer to just disappear.

Carrie's period signifying the beginning of her powers and the end for her small town is gross. Similarly, *The Exorcist*'s protagonist Regan, a wayward twelve-year-old girl who swears, masturbates, pisses on the floor and is deemed to be possessed, is a prime example of how young women become symbols for grossness in popular culture. Off-screen, I underwent my own transformation into a fully fledged gross girl due to my disability, making the theoretical and symbolic implications of being gross central to understanding my identity. But being outwardly gross also signals a complete rejection of social norms, of our societal stereotypes, and of the patriarchal order of the world. Being gross isn't just about being open about the disgusting things that happen to us on the inside, but also being entirely unafraid of who we are on the outside.

Marginalised people are told so often that we are too much – too loud, too visible and taking up too much space. We expect women to be happy with their lot; to remain quiet, to behave properly and to not question their surroundings. Essentially, if a femme is acting in a way we don't expect, she is gross. Horror lays bare the most extreme form of grossness, combining the repulsiveness of our bodily functions with actions deemed evil and immoral irrespective of motive. In these stories and the on-screen world of horror films, a physical revulsion for our leading ladies establishes a woman's true identity, whether that be a possessed monster, a telekinetic teenager, a vampire, werewolf, succubus or any other form of other-worldly evil.

Our innate disgust towards anything gross paired with a femme acting in a traditionally uncouth manner frames these characters and identities as the ones we've been taught are traditionally terrifying. While the original intent is surely to put us in our rightful place – to paint wayward femininity as the eventual downfall of our universe and scare women into keeping their mouths shut – watching these depictions had the opposite effect on me. With no concrete representation for those disabled, chronically ill or fat, I was forced to look elsewhere for people I could relate to. In doing so, I realised that these characters aren't simply evil; their emotions and ideas have been suppressed, like so many of ours have. Depictions of gross behaviour in the horror genre, be it Carrie's revenge, Regan's rebellion or any other number of female characters twisting the knife on feminine stereotypes, simply demonstrate a rejection of patriarchal norms at their most extreme.

*

As I gorged on stories in which women act in the exact opposite way to how we are taught, I realised it wasn't only the initial shock and jump scares of the genre that kept me replaying these depictions of wayward femininity. What drew me to the tales of good girls gone bad was that their transformations did not signal linear growth in the ways we've come to expect from our protagonists. These characters weren't getting better; in fact, they were becoming villains in their own right. Other films showed their leads in some way or another assimilating with what the world expects women to be: becoming academically successful, conventionally attractive, or settling down with their romantic interest. We've all watched with glee as the high-school nerd peels off her glasses and is whisked off to prom by the school's sweetheart, when the lovable under-achiever is accepted into an Ivy League college, and the intern climbs the career ladder all the way to CEO, smashing the patriarchy on her ascent to success.

But in the case of horror films, the fear that others feel for them as these women refuse to conform often fuels change – and these teen girls rip up the world as they know it to start afresh. What I found missing across other genres, and in other female protagonists, wasn't due to a lack of variety in the stories being told. I've watched women on screen be sad, mourn, climb the career ladder, save a lab of entrapped chihuahuas, fall out with friends and start families, but one single facet of the human experience was absent from nearly every other representation of woman-hood contained in a two-hour film. Rage. Rage that can't be subdued at the bottom of a litre of ice cream, or washed away with enough margaritas to sink a small ship. Rage that boils in the pit of your stomach, unfiltered by a good story-line or colour grading. The rage that marginalised people so often feel but have no idea what to do with.

From birth, cisgender straight white men have the luxury of watching their own dark emotions parroted on our screens. If they wish to, they can watch themselves murder, kill, manipulate, run organised crime rings, commit fraud and ruin families. Not only that, but we're also exposed to endless rationalisations as to why men behave in these ways. Women and marginalised people not only do not have the representation they deserve, but the absence of a mirror held up by the world has real implications for our emotions and what we feel we can do with them. We have no framework for where our rage can go, what it can do, or the implications of unleashing it. Through not seeing these emotions reflected back at us in popular culture, women learn to consider the implications of our anger. We're forced to think more deeply about how to use it, and become covert in how we channel our negative thoughts and emotions.

Watching *Carrie*, the 1976 film adaptation of Stephen King's novel, was possibly the first time I witnessed a woman fully release, and realise, the entirety of her rage.

Following our teen protagonist through her hellish high-school experience, we watch as Carrie experiences her telekinetic powers for the first time as her period begins. Seeing her story play out on screen – and her menstruation result in all-out destruction – I began to realise that what goes on in our bodies is inexplicably bound up with a fear of disruption of patriarchal society. Carrie's sexuality, puberty and power are intrinsically tied together through-out her story. Meek, oppressed by her mother and bullied at school, she is a character who wields no power when we first meet her. Slowly but surely, whether it be through her transformation into womanhood or the strengthening of her supernatural gifts, she begins to realise her power, disobeying her fundamentalist Christian mother, exploring desire, and eventually ripping apart her prom, her school and her entire town.

Carrie's story is meant to be a cautionary tale of what happens when young womanhood gets out of hand and sexuality is left unchecked. It is one of thousands of stories we consume on a near-daily basis that aims to other the experiences of anyone who isn't a cis-het white man. A woman's more likely role within the horror genre is as a victim – to sexual aggression, violence or monsters.

Classic slasher films such as *Scream*, *A Nightmare on Elm Street*, *Halloween* and *The Texas Chainsaw Massacre* – to name but a few – all position men as monsters with the ability to subject the world to their pain, with women as the people who have to run from it. If we're lucky, we may find one gorgeous girl surviving the wrath of the script and making it through the closing credits by the skin of her teeth. Both narrative tropes – those that place women as victims, and those that place them as aggressors – build upon decades of literature, film and other audience-facing representation that urges marginalised people to stay in line and accept their place in society.

The difference between stories that surrender their femme characters to evil forces and the ones whose female protagonists enact evil is simple: the former are victims to an already unfair society, while the latter work to change it through whatever powers they can wield. The withdrawn, silent Carrie who understands her place as secondary in the world felt far more scary to me than her murderous, uncontrollable transformation into full telekinetic, supernatural force who kills her bullies and shuns her family.

As the VHS whirled in its player, through these films I began to realise the power in difference. When I felt isolated from the world, the stories of fictional young women undergoing their own metamorphosis provided me with the power to realise the infinite possibilities that come with embracing the facets of ourselves that others fear.

On first viewings, I struggled with the idea that these young women were acting as detrimental to the worlds they lived in. Watching them rip up and disrupt everything around them, we're often left to infer what will remain of society once the end credits start rolling. What I did know for sure was that these characters left their stories more wholly formed, and with more autonomy, than when they started them. The complexity of characters who find it difficult to curtail their emotions – whether physically or mentally – matched my own experiences far more closely than a perfectly dressed leading lady going through the motions of trying to make it in the city, suburb, career or social class of her choosing. Our horror heroines' actions may disrupt, but disruption is not necessarily a negative thing. When considering that these overt displays of violence, disorder and abjectness often lead to a person's true identity being formed through narrative structures, the implication that the world before was a functioning one is a farce.

Just like the rest of us, women in horror films live under the patriarchy, experiencing ableism, racism and inequality. Much of their desire to disrupt comes from a discontentment with the status quo; something that I particularly connected to as a discontented teen. The wider world of feminine representation on screen is traditionally one in which individual characters solve their individual problems: dating, desire, family, work, body issues. I learned that in Hollywood, there's nothing a good makeover cannot fix. In horror, before their monstrous alter egos are revealed, the genre's leading ladies are entrenched in the same societal expectations that we all are – the ones that make our bodies terrifying to inhabit. Through their transformation, and informed by the restrictions and expectations placed upon their existence, these women can work to undo the wrongs of the world, using their new-found powers to shatter all illusions of stereotypically perfect femininity.

For the most part, these protagonists look exactly like the women we're taught to regard as acceptably sexual: white, skinny, blonde and beautiful. Watching their bodies transform into monstrosities felt akin to my own body self-destructing during diagnosis, though a crucial point of difference sits uncomfortably between me and these protagonists. Their beauty allows audiences six degrees of separation between their characters and the real world, meaning their existence is never as tangibly disgusting as my own.

While I'm completely fascinated by these characters' unwillingness to hide the unsavoury facets of their exist-ence, be they physical or emotional, the fact that they are afforded the space to be outwardly abject is undeniably linked to their desirability in the wider world. Putting their beauty aside, I am far more interested in exploring how these women's deplorable bodily functions construct physicality and disgust as a form of power. On the other hand, the revulsion and fear that arise from someone's body acting out of place are aspects of existence that have not yet been enveloped by capitalism's tight grip. In reality, disability, fatness, gender nonconformity, race and other marginalised parts of existence are either desexualised or fetishised for those who struggle to understand them.

Tales of menstrual teens continue to fascinate audiences and filmmakers alike, with stories such as *Carrie* and *Ginger Snaps* (which chronicles a teenage girl becoming a werewolf in sync with her first period) remaining popular, though gender-essentialist, narratives for young women trying to understand their bodies. As important as they were to me individually – pre-Crohn's disease, when my period was the most monstrous thing I could imagine – as they have been to many others, these narratives simply do not represent the wide scope of identity that is crucial to modern feminism, and ignores those who may not correlate their bodily functions with their gender. In the case of disability, my body may behave in ways that make me feel hopeless, but through this comes an immense power: the power to confuse a world that only accepts an empowered woman when she acts within the parameters of usefulness to society.

Society has no script on how to deal with a fat, chronically ill woman in her twenties who refuses to accept invisibility. Because of that, the potential to write my own narrative is infinite. As I entered adulthood, I naively expected that the freedom of growing up would grant me the ability to apply all the power I gleaned from these characters to my own gross existence. As the seeds of fourth-wave feminism were planted, I felt hopeful that the ability to communicate the complexity of my emotions would become second nature – not only for myself, but for my whole generation. I turned away from the horror genre feeling equipped to take on the realities of womanhood.

Across the world, our lived experiences quickly became increasingly fraught. We no longer needed horror films to induce a quick, adrenaline-shooting scare. But as our own universe becomes darker, I believe there is a lot we can learn from onscreen anti-heroines who embrace their grossness. Sadly, contemporary feminism has no room for bitches or gross girls. #NastyWomen may have once trended, becoming a rallying cry for women's rights in the wake of Trump's 2016 election campaign, but our ability to embrace the full spectrum of our emotions, attitudes and bodies is arguably as narrow as ever.

Fiction has had its own dalliances with evil, ushering in unlikeable women in titles such as *Gone Girl*, *Sharp Objects*, *Little Fires Everywhere* and more. But this brief obsession with the idea of feminine manipulation did little to push forward acceptance of any tangible grossness in the real world. While this minor cultural moment may have failed to create ripples beyond our pages and screens, representation of our rage, regardless of intention or conse-quence, helps create a more nuanced depiction of our lives. Not due to the expression of anger itself, but to the fact that by excluding these portrayals of unsavoury experiences, we are further boxing marginalised people into narrow stereotypes and standards that restrict our existences. Without accepting the good, the bad and the ugly of our emotions, the ability for us to move forward progressively is limited.

In the last half-decade, the fight for equal rights has been depoliticised. The generation that grew up with the Spice Girls – my generation – reached full maturity, and girl power made a comeback like never before. Our modern feminist influencers are now more likely to present as the cardboard cut-outs of feminine stereotypes that we've been conditioned to aspire to for years. Scrolling through Instagram conjures up the same adolescent longing I once felt for a more well-rounded, gross depiction of woman-hood. Like the protagonists in my favourite horror films, these women are nearly always white, undeniably beauti-ful, able-bodied and either skinny or #blessed with perfect Kardashian curves.

Those who now dominate the widespread conversation around contemporary feminism are as backwardly aspira-tional as any model found on the runway. Unlike in films, we expect our modern feminist spokespeople to be like us. They aren't traditional celebrities or academic scholars; they're people with Instagram accounts. In the case of horror, a cinema screen and a tightly edited script sepa-rated my existence from those who populated my fictional worlds; and I accepted the fact that the female characters

I resonated with would probably never fully represent my existence – they were made up. However, that same sheen does not apply to feminist influencers.

Feminist influencers are people we can imagine going to the pub with, and who we watch as their lives unfold as if they're a close friend. We convince ourselves that these young women could seamlessly slot into our lives. Their relatability doesn't come from the fact that more of us see ourselves in them than the previous powerful figures we've been spoon-fed. Rather, their perfection is paired with insistence that they are in fact as subversively flawed as the rest of us. Through self-editing, and Instagram, these young people toe the line of being just enough like us that they feel like our friends, while remaining distinctly perfect; a pristine vision of the 'right kind of woman'. Their feed posts – usually either graphic pink squares paired with an empowering quote, or perfectly poised selfies – urge us to dump our boyfriends, accept our sagging bodies, and that our emotions are normal.

But the feelings these people urge us to accept are not the ones we've been taught are deeply shameful. Rather, the hang-ups and societal ideas they peddle as damaging are simply a symptom of the parts of ourselves we've learned to hide since birth. They want us to self-improve out of any darkness we've been keeping inside; on a singular level that focuses on personal improvement over structural change. To 'unlearn' internalised misogyny and mental health problems – as if we have manifested them largely on our own terms and not as a by-product of inequality. As marginalised people, we can only learn from one another that we have the power to find our own strength. Through community care, this can be successful.

But in the world of influence, we're setting up an unachievable narrative of aspiration that prioritises marketability under a patriarchal distribution of capitalism and brand wealth. From the word go, our grossness has never been something that is seen as worthy of investment or self-respect, and no amount of work on ourselves will change that. In placing the onus on each one of us to solve society's issues, our unlikeable qualities become more taboo. If we're not seen to be moving at an upwards trajectory online, we're disposable.

Though not deliberate, this rhetoric puts Insta(nt)-gratification before meaningful change, and scrubs away the idea that any sort of abjection could be beneficial to the movement. The easily digestible nature of these accounts and influencers strips feminism of any type of complex emotion. By simplifying our confusion, frustration or outright anger, we're wrapping our complexities up in pretty pink bows and erasing them from existence. These accounts provide some light relief from the dangers of the real world, convincing us that there is perhaps more hope and solidarity than we believe, while sprinkling in enough social justice to lull us into a false sense of forward progression.

We've sought to normalise the gross facets of ourselves for which we are ostracised under the guise of 'acceptability', diluting any political urgency in the fight for equal rights. But while searching to be understood, we've managed to sanitise our often ugly experiences. Social media campaigns urge us to reach out, speak up and be kind. We're encouraged to temper our arguments in order to be taken seriously, to support one another unconditionally, and to exercise restraint when calling out injustice. In doing so, we're removing the physical and emotional messiness and grossness that comes from our experiences.

The past half-decade has seen a huge shift in rhetoric towards destigmatising what we are marginalised for: mental health, body image, menstruation and more. The commodification of our sadness leaves no room for nuance. Instead, our mental health issues have been made over with an unsavoury tweeness that locks any semblance of grossness out of sight and out of mind. The intricacies of our lives become yet another thing that can be solved through buying products or following the right person, and in doing so our rallying cries become nothing but a whimper.

With the rise of social media, marginalised people have been offered the opportunity to write their own narratives, shine a spotlight on their experiences and destigmatise the aspects of our existences that have long been erased.

However, the online world still only allows 2D depictions of our 3D lives. As we adapt ourselves in pursuit of personal branding, our hang-ups, flaws and the ability to fight for what we believe in become flattened. Through this quest for acceptance – and popularity – on the internet, we're encouraged to place our differences front and centre. And often to focus on only one facet of ourselves.

If every marginalised person with a social media account that leans towards the sociopolitical was a legitimate politician, we'd be single-issue candidates. Focusing on one single fact of marginalisation is lucrative: if our identities can be neatly packaged into a social media bio or perfectly curated feed, our follower count is likely to increase tenfold. Following the lead of those who have carved out careers by becoming self-appointed spokespeople for the oppressed – a poster child for body positivity, a specific mental health diagnosis, or the shittiness of dating as a femme – is now a legitimate career option. While we all try to work out our niches and which aspect of our insecurity to hone in on, marginalised people aren't seen as multifaceted human beings.

Where horror film anti-heroines use their rage to force change within their universe – or in some cases destroy it entirely – my generation instead capitalises on victimhood. The parts of ourselves we've been oppressed for become backwards badges of honour, with influencers catering to a privileged gaze in an attempt to be understood in their oppression as opposed to dismantling it altogether. Their rhetoric focuses on how unfair things are, in a way that always frames marginalised identities as underdogs to be pitied, without offering tangible solutions beyond buying into their sponsored content. For many people, our trauma is near impossible to translate to personal branding; it cannot be overcome, taught away or exercised out of. There is no getting over it.

This quest to be marketable, relatable, representative of an underprivileged group *and* politically astute means that those who more directly fall in line with our current societal standards rise to the top. Those whose troubles are not as marketable or easily understood are left behind. We find ourselves back in the same position I felt as a teenager, pretending that my own darkness didn't exist and desperately trying to be understood in spite of it. Current conversations around feminism place ultimate value on things that make us feel good, whether that's empathising with someone less privileged through engaging with their content, or seeking acceptance from our peers via our own. In reality, our lived experiences are often not neatly digestible via content created for a social media platform; meaning those who most need to access these ideas feel more shut out than ever before.

Growing up, watching these young people behave in a completely different way from anything I had ever seen before felt empowering. However, once I was diagnosed with my chronic health condition, my relationship with grossness became both more tangible and a little more complicated. More often than not, my own body feels like a monster; my Crohn's disease often means my body and its functions are utterly alien to me. My stomach cramps can find me doubled over in pain on the pavement. Imagining my own rotting organs, repulsive in and of themselves, does not feel powerful. I've seen pictures of my insides that more closely resemble scenes from one of the horror films I grew up on than a normal digestive system.

Society views disabled people – whether that disability is physical or otherwise – as monstrous. We disrupt normality. The same fear that empowered my changing body as a teenager came to oppress my disabled corporeal form as a young adult. It's hard to find the symbolic power in being gross when you find yourself living it every single day. My theoretical interest in feminine disgust became a very real one; one that would find me throwing up outside bus stops in suburban English towns at ten o'clock in the morning. Not because I'd drunk too much the night before, but because my own insides were trying to kill me. Witnessing the very real rejection and horror from bystanders who refused to help cemented the taboo nature of, and reaction to, marginalised people. People who – just by existing as who they are – aren't behaving as they should

. My disability, despite being largely invisible, has altered people's perceptions of me far more than my femininity ever has.

In the midst of fourth-wave feminism, I felt more isolated from my body than ever before. Disabled people are left outside the margins of acceptability that dominate social-media-based feminism, along with those whose struggles may not be as directly relatable as our thirty-day cycle. As the fight for equality becomes consumed by easily understood messages, individualism and aesthetics, the question of how we can dismantle the patriarchy through collective power becomes irrelevant. While social media is focused on forms of empowerment to help women assimilate into already rotten power structures, I knew I would never be able to find a place in them. What a move towards acceptability signals is not a deconstruction of the power structures that have kept us down, but rather an upholding of them under the guise of a society perceived as more equal. As the fight for equal rights permeates capitalism, business and social circles, the function of feminism as we understand it becomes diluted.

Normalising our perceived imperfections only serves those whose personal horror can be concealed or, if the Instagram influencers have their way, diminished. Many of us deal with an existence that will never be considered normal under the current stereotypes upheld by society. In my experience as a marginalised person, if your anger is too visible, you're difficult. If you're fat, you're unhealthy, unattractive and a strain on our healthcare system. If you're disabled, or chronically ill, you'll either be pitied or patronised. One of the things I struggled with most when diagnosed with Crohn's disease was the fact that I was no longer deemed productive to society. I feared job interviews, would become anxious when friends reacted to my experiences with well-meaning sadness, and counted down the days until my next inevitable act of public abasement would rear its ugly head.

When I most needed it, returning to watching these horror films helped me feel less alone. They served as a reminder that my own grossness was something to be celebrated, despite the fact that it couldn't be normalised. Though physical transformations and explicit depictions of a marginalised body's ability to scare drew a closer parallel to my own experiences as I grew into adulthood, I was also deeply obsessed with 'evil' female characters whose nastiness manifested in their minds rather than their bodies. This is a fascination that has carried me into full maturity as a human. This facet of the horror genre helped me understand how women can be complicit in the upholding of inequality, even if their motives appear forward-thinking.

I am still obsessed with characters like Veronica Sawyer, from the eighties teen film turned horror *Heathers*, who kills off her popular peers one by one in order to create a more equal high-school hierarchy. Stories like *Heathers* position their protagonists as undermining a society that is skewed against those who are marginalised, and as women who have simply had enough of containing the evil inside of them. *Midsommar*, the 2019 pagan-horror flick, sees protagonist Dani opt to burn her shitty boyfriend alive following his gaslighting and manipulative behaviour. Sofia Coppola's 2017 period drama *The Beguiled* follows a group of women as they torture an American Civil War soldier as a release for their own frustration, and *Gone Girl* (first a novel by Gillian Flynn, then adapted for the big screen by David Fincher in 2014) has us watching Amy Dunne fuck up her husband's life as retribution for men's inability to process women as multi-faceted human beings.

Watching these women manipulate, lie and kill provides a different emotional experience to watching a character who starts her story at the mercy of her bodily functions but learns how to use them to her advantage. Seeing women on screen enact violence against those who have oppressed them is a cathartic revelation; it demonstrates our frustration in ways we have likely never been able to experience in the real world. In these films we see untempered femmes grappling with the unfairness of their lives, encountering behaviour towards them that many of us have been taught is normal. Gaslighting, emotional abuse and bullying are all things marginalised people have come to expect as a day-to-day reality of existence, but these characters refuse to accept the cards they've been dealt.

They match patriarchal evil with their own darkest fantasies, proving that our pain does not have to make us victims. While it is momentarily revelatory to see these characters confront their oppressors head-on, such depictions are not necessarily worthy of being put on a pedestal. These women's actions also demonstrate that when oppressed people feel hidden or ignored, they are capable of inflicting their own violence and hurt onto others. While their behaviour may be extreme, it demonstrates a level of autonomy rarely afforded to marginalised identities. It's difficult to not relate to their desperation, and it's important to have representation for those who do act within extremities.

Men aren't the sole perpetrators of oppression, which our current feminist hellscape demonstrates. As the way we engage with social media becomes more complicated and all-encompassing of only individual emancipation, it's arguably now easier than ever to cause each other harm or erase each other's existence. The ways in which women hurt one another are rarely as simple or straightforward as a murderous horror spree or supernatural disaster. Our actions are often intricate and subconscious. Without this representation of the damage we are capable of, there is no honest conversation about how we can achieve equality. To challenge these power structures we must first understand them. Once we accept our place in upholding the patriarchal order, including the denial of our own horrible grossness, we can begin to pull it apart.

While recounting our individual traumas for the consumption of anyone with a social media account may make us more inward-facing than ever, there is the opportunity to seek out different stories and tales of marginalisation that we may not directly relate to. Contemporary feminism is waking up to individual responsibilities and privileges, with learning resources easier to access than ever before. How we process our own actions, and then apply these teachings effectively on a wider community-based scale, is yet to be accurately realised. While our horror heiresses may be beacons of conventional beauty, in reality, women of colour, disabled women, transgender women and women who don't conform to Westernised standards are far more likely to be brutalised in addition to being demonised by society.

When faced with something monstrous – whether that's our own inner feelings, or someone else's experiences that we don't understand – we are likely to retreat further into ourselves and how we can be harmed by it. The search for understanding of self means we rarely seek to deconstruct the conditions that have made us who we are, the graces we've been afforded or who we have ignored throughout that journey. Accepting how other identities are individually demonised can be perceived as giving up some of our own victimhood; it's often easier to disregard someone's entire existence than accept they are worse off than us. Victimhood in the world of horror anti-heroines provides women with the emotional break required to change their circumstances. In twenty-first-century feminism, victimhood is the cultural capital that provides us with cachet – rewarding us with followers, social status and even money to pay our bills.

Only through accepting the full nastiness of our world, and our own complicity within it, can we move forward progressively towards a more equal society. While we choose to only embrace the parts of ourselves that are easily changeable and willing to be loved, the likelihood of anyone understanding our experiences will be curbed. We need a full-on overhaul of our politics, or lack thereof. But with femmes thirsty for blood already running rampant across our TV screens and within the pages of our books, by taking our expressions of anger into the IRL world we may just have a fighting chance at moving feminism forward.

In the wake of being diagnosed, the thought of being handed an incurable illness felt like the worst thing that could possibly happen to me. However, being faced with a new, disgusting part of myself that would never disappear helped me realise that all of us live with unspoken rules that stop us from accepting the unsavoury facets of our own lives. In the struggle for acceptance – not only on a world-wide level, but on a personal one too – we slowly squirrel away the parts of ourselves we think others won't like.

Diagnosed with a disability, this became an impossibility. I was forced to accept the worst things my own body could do to me, that normality was no longer an option, and that I would be considered monstrous – even on a subconscious level – by both those close to me and society at large. The things we consider to be the worst parts of ourselves are not necessarily the ones we should be ashamed of.

Our true identities may be sometimes unsavoury, difficult to understand or even impossible to like, but that doesn't mean we should ignore them. By embracing these things rather than burying them, we can come to understand ourselves better. If we refuse to allow ourselves to be softened and censored under misogynistic portrayals of female empowerment, we can force out the empowerment-lite dominating our culture, our minds and our social media feeds. If equality is truly the goal, we must accept that the gross girl inside us is impossible to avoid, and to embrace her is to ask for more than the meek promise of acceptance could ever provide us with.

Self-love is a lie

The universality of self-loathing is the reason why the allure of body positivity is so potent. Without dismantling fatphobia, being bigger will always exist as a fear which wriggles its way into skinny people's minds.

Self-love is something that has never come naturally to me. Some days, I don't hate the way I look. I'm fat, and although I have felt as though I was overweight my whole life, that is not the case. The days spent pinching my stomach and chugging down weight-loss shakes during my teens were fruitless; I was a very average size 10–12 and nothing could be done to shift it. Like most women, I have been taught that my body isn't OK, and that I should always strive to optimise it through exercise, dietary choices and faddy products promising that a shift in body size will cure my brain of all its ills. Even at a 'normal' size, growing up, I rarely saw anyone beyond a size 6 appear on my favourite TV shows or in culture at large – and if they did catch some screen time, they were being mocked. My generation grew up idolising lollipop-headed celebrities, bearing witness to society's obsession with extremely skinny women and obsessively scanning the circles of shame in weekly celeb magazines.

What I did not realise was that all those hours spent hating my body would one day be entirely pointless. That one day I would wake up and have a legitimate reason for all the rage I felt towards the skin and bones that made me: my body was trying to kill me. My diagnosis with Crohn's disease occurred during the time I looked the best I ever had but felt worse than I could have imagined. For the first time since childhood, I could see my ribs outlined on my body, people were complimenting my figure, and I began to generally worry less about how I was being perceived by others.

At the same time, I was becoming increasingly unwell, unable to keep food down and frequently spotting blood in the toilet bowl. I never correlated my declining health with losing weight; why would I? All my life I had been told that being thin meant being healthy, attractive and desirable. I may have struggled to go a full day without vomiting due to the bubbling nausea overwhelming my senses, but I rationalised my shrinking waistline as being a result of walking more and living independently for the first time – rather than the fact that my immune system was ravaging my digestive organs from the inside out.

While my teen years co-existed alongside some of the most brutal messaging women have ever experienced regarding their bodies, as I adapted to chronically ill life, body positivity entered the picture. Online, I saw people my age embracing their flaws and pulling apart the beauty standards that have been woven into our consciousness over the last century. As my generation grew into adulthood, we decided enough was enough, and spearheaded a movement intent on loving yourself no matter how you look. Armed with the first ever iPhone, marginalised people began photographing the bits they'd previously been taught to hate about themselves, posting their bodies alongside pithy quotes that alluded to the negative impact of speaking or thinking badly of your own image.

Body positivity – from its early inception online right up to the present day – has always focused on the self. How we, individually, feel about our bodies and their shortcomings as opposed to the treatment of those who fall outside conventional beauty on a societal level. As a teenager or young person, this makes sense – there isn't a single marginalised person in the world who didn't feel shitty about how they looked while growing up. Whether skinny, fat or somewhere in between, growing up in the 2000s, your body was put under a magnifying glass. Watching others openly admit their own insecurities and then deconstruct them piece by piece felt liberating at the time. The inception of body positivity existed in a sociopolitical soup that also encompassed racial politics, class politics and feminism. Coming to more deeply understand all these things at once felt like an awakening, and an opportunity to rebuild how marginalised people are treated on a wider level than simply the thoughts in our own heads. I found body positivity at a moment in time when I truly needed it; when my own form felt completely alien.

As quickly as I lost the weight, I put it back on. Treatment for Crohn's disease often involves long courses of steroids, which I was administered first by drip straight into my veins, followed by an elongated course of oral tablets spanning multiple months. During the first year of my diagnosis, I went through this treatment twice. One of its most common side effects is weight gain. My face puffed up, my stomach filled out and my bones were once again cushioned by soft fat. I was not just carrying water weight from the steroids, but slowly morphing back to the body I would probably have always grown into had I not become gravely unwell.

Gaining weight due to medication or recovery from illness, in my experience, is not a slow and steady process. My entire body and face shape changed overnight. Without access to body positivity rhetoric online, I probably would have spiralled into complete misery over my new appearance. Instead, I posted selfies, experimented with make-up and embraced my new body. Avoiding a full-blown identity crisis, I could see what piling on the pounds really meant – and that my changing exterior signalled the internal healing my body was undertaking. My perspective entirely shifted; I could no longer spend hours obsessing over my appearance and had to focus on what my body had been through and managing my new condition. Instead of avoiding mirrors, constructing my identity became a source of joy. I no longer felt restricted by what I should or should not wear as dictated by body types made up for magazine features.

I spent the hottest months of the year – usually a period

of dread in which I'd cover my flesh in thick tights and long sleeves, sweating buckets but afraid to expose my body – running around in crop tops, cutting my hair short and revelling in the fact that I was getting better. I had always thought my life would begin once I was skinny, that suddenly all my hang-ups would disappear and I would emerge as the butterfly I was born to be. Years of hearing phrases such as 'inside every fat person is a skinny person screaming to get out' had buried fatphobia deep into my psyche, and I truly believed that to be happy I had to change how I looked. In actuality, I experienced the exact opposite. Once I realised that gaining weight directly correlated to an increase in my overall quality of life, everything changed. I developed more empathy for myself as well as those around me, and could see our cultural markers of beauty for the restrictive, reductive and redundant rules they really are.

The blissful honeymoon period I experienced with my new body size didn't last. In the years since that first summer, my relationship with how I look has hardened and my attitude towards body positivity is infinitely more cynical. Self-love is now a global phenomenon. The beach-body-ready marketing I grew up with is a thing of the past; women with washboard abs and perfect blow-dries no longer taunt us from their perfectly lit advertisements on the side of the Tube. On the surface, our fetishistic attitude towards skinniness has shifted, as even the most high-end fashion brands with the worst old-school attitudes begin to introduce 'curve' models onto the catwalk.

Lyrics in pop songs focus on cultivating a healthy relationship with yourself rather than pining for lost love or chronicling the first inklings of lust. Entire industries intent on cashing in on our insecurities have switched gears, and now offer their services or products under the premise of helping us to like ourselves more authentically. Even Weight Watchers, a brand synonymous with diet culture and weight loss, has rebranded to WW. With a new tagline declaring that they offer 'wellness that works', the company has shifted towards a model that supposedly prioritises overall wellness and healthy living rather than the size of your waist. We're urged at every turn to embrace our flaws, and are suddenly expected to love the parts of ourselves we've been conditioned to hate.

We have reached peak body positivity. While this should simplify our relationships with our bodies, the concept of beauty has never been more conflicted. While outwardly it may appear as though we have progressed forward with a widely accepted more liberal mindset when it comes to body image, self-love is little more than smoke and mirrors. Cloaked in the language of progressive politics but still peddling the same damaging ideologies, our attitudes to what is or is not beautiful have in fact become more conservative. A marginal amount of acceptance for diverse bodies has been incorporated into our everyday lives, but only as long as you adhere to the specific set of acceptable flaws outlined by the same authorities that taught us to resent ourselves in the first place.

Beauty and fashion brands may be emphasising the importance of loving ourselves, but the British government and society at large has differing ideas. During the COVID-19 pandemic, Prime Minister Boris Johnson declared a war on obesity, placing the pressure on obese individuals to overhaul their lifestyle or face the burden of blame for Britain's death toll due to the pandemic. Once the vaccine rollout began, and fat people were prioritised for inoculation, public outrage piled on as to why those who refused to look after their health were jumping the queue for medication that could save all our lives. This government-sanctioned fatphobia leads to a downward spiral in quality of life for all fat people; it makes us depressed, it subjects us to street harassment or online abuse, and it tells us we aren't worthy of a happy existence.

Where I once felt pride in my body, as my symptoms have plateaued but with my BMI still rising, I struggle to feel the enthusiasm for my frame that I once did. There is a long history of research that proves weight does not necessarily correlate to health. Unfit skinny people have been proven to develop diabetes at double the rate of healthy fat people, and the BMI scale was invented by a mathematician, not a scientist. Despite the belief that losing weight will save us all, there are studies dating back to 1959 finding that 98 per cent of weight-loss attempts fail, with the majority of those who do diet gaining back more weight than they lost in the long run. Other studies have found that up to three quarters of obese people are in fact metabolically healthy.

In my own experience, I was at my most unwell when I weighed the least, and at one point in my life, I was the most healthy I could be but the largest I ever had been. However, I cannot say the same about myself today. I am not a healthy woman; I live with chronic illness. Optimum health is something that is physically impossible for me to achieve. Putting my medical condition to one side, the way I live my life isn't healthy – but then nor are the lifestyles of so many of my thin friends. We all drink, order takeaways and avoid exercising for months on end. But none of the aforementioned lifestyle choices mean that I – or any other fat person – deserve disrespect.

By accepting fat people only on the condition that they are also healthy, an entire intersection of those like myself who will never be able to ring up a perfect bill of health are left by the wayside. While skinny, or not quite fat, people may experience days on which they feel absolutely awful about how they look, their morality as a human being isn't tied to the food they eat or their ability to prove that their choices do not negatively impact their health. It's natural to one day hate yourself and the next believe you are absolutely the most beautiful being to ever grace this earth. All our relationships with how we look fluctuate. But body positivity has only come to put more pressure on those most marginalised to feel good about themselves, with little real external change in terms of the actual acceptance of their bodies that is required to help them to do so.

Body positivity and our attitude to fatness has not always existed in a vacuum of individualism, nor is it a new concept pioneered by soap brands. Our concept of personal liberation is so fragmented from political activism that the idea of people taking to the streets to protest how fat people are treated seems almost fever-dream-like. But that is exactly how the fat acceptance movement first started, in the late sixties, with a sit-in – or, as described then, a fat-in – in New York City's Central Park. Protesting against the bias fat people faced in society, a group of people burned diet books and pictures of Twiggy, brandished signs that read 'Take a fat girl to dinner' and took up space as unapologetically fat individuals, working as a group towards emancipation.

Shortly afterwards, in 1967, the first piece of fat-positive writing appeared in an American publication, written by Llewellyn Louderback and entitled 'More People Should Be FAT'. As the relevance and public awareness of these issues grew, the first official fat activist communities were born. Shortly after its inception in 1969, the National Association to Advance Fat Acceptance started a letter-writing campaign in order to connect fat people across

America. Informed and inspired by the feminist and gay rights movements, fat people began campaigning for rights on a civil basis, pushing their needs as a societal issue and exposing the oppression of larger bodies across society. As the politics of fat acceptance gained traction, more activist groups popped up, becoming increasingly radical as time went on.

This collective groundswell of conversation resulted in works such as the Fat Liberation Manifesto of 1973, created by LA based activists the Fat Underground. Coining the phrase 'Diets are a cure that doesn't work for a disease that doesn't exist', and peddling slogans such as 'Change society, not ourselves', and 'Doctors are the enemy. Weight loss is genocide', the collective focused on weight control as a tool for population oppression, arguing that many psychological issues surrounding our bodies were born out of the idea that we should control what we eat and how we look. The manifesto itself marked the first time fat people were called upon to unify under a common purpose: to raise awareness of, and break down, how society discriminated against their bodies.

The timeline of the fat liberation movement largely runs parallel with the waves of feminism, with each informing and crossing paths with the other. Historically, fat activism has been a woman's fight. That's not to say that fatphobia is a problem solely confined to women; more that historically we have been the focus of cultural beauty standards and brainwashing. At the movement's inception, fat acceptance was spearheaded by plus-size men fighting against the oppression their wives faced, with women then starting to lead the way alongside feminism's second wave. Over time, the movement diverged from heteronormativity, with queer women revolutionising conversations around fatness through radical activism.

Crucially, fat acceptance has always run parallel to other social justice movements, with many fat activists figuring out their feelings on fatness within the context of queerness, race or gender before embarking on their own movement. This resulted in fat acceptance being viewed through the lens of intersectionality rather than an issue existing in its own bubble, and therefore allowed the movement to penetrate conversations surrounding social justice. In the early eighties, fat swims were organised by lesbian activists, and Audre Lorde's *Zami: A New Spelling of My Name* referred to the beauty of fat Black women not in spite of their body weight, but because of it. In 1984, Grace Nichols released her poetry collection *The Fat Black Woman's Poems*, which became a seminal text for the movement, due to lines such as 'Beauty / is a fat black woman'.

In the late eighties, the London Fat Women's Group was formed out of the Women's Centre, with the aim of forging ties and understanding the links between fatness and other marginalised identities. Despite workplace bias on weight being ruled illegal by a federal court of America in 1993, forging policy changes in the field of fat acceptance has been slow and largely unfruitful. As the nineties went on, fat acceptance morphed into a movement more cultural in nature than overtly or traditionally political. While still pushing similar yet evolving ideologies, the focus of fat acceptance switched gear towards zines such as *FAT!SO?*, as well as literature and club nights. This step into popular culture paved the way for fat acceptance blogs, fat influencers, and the discussion of body size becoming more widespread than ever before. Though online communities initially focused on the rights and fights of fat women, these spaces on the internet eventually paved the way for modern body positivity as we know it today.

Because body image issues affect each and every one of us, the rhetoric around self-love being a personal plight, related to one's individual attitude, has slowly eroded any radicalism the original roots of the movement once possessed. The intersectionality pioneered in earlier movements has been replaced by an all-encompassing focus on feeling that ignores the real societal biases that put us here in the first place. While body positivity has ensured we all feel the immense pressure to accept ourselves for who we are without modification, those who peddle the message of self-love are often the same vision of beauty we've been force-fed for the last century. Embracing their barely-there flaws, influencers and celebrities quite literally bend over backwards to show us enforced, unnatural tummy rolls, unflattering angles and the power of good lighting in completely over-hauling whether a selfie is deemed ugly or attractive.

A-listers preach the power of accepting and loving your-self for who you are in the captions of Instagram posts featuring heavily face-tuned filters that render the celeb-rity barely recognisable from their 'natural' self. In doing this, the chasm of acceptance between those who feel ugly sometimes and those who are continually told they are unattractive by society widens and widens. Although body positivity can have an impact on intersections of identity beyond fatness – for example, race and disability – the mes-saging often centres on those who most traditionally feel fine about themselves: white, somewhat slim, able-bodied cisgender women.

This may have increased such people's self-confidence, but it ensures that those most marginalised based on image are pushed further and further away from critical conver-sations. While it is true that we all suffer body hang-ups and low self-esteem, and that women are more highly scrutinised based on their image alone, not all women are systematically oppressed based on their appearance. Fat women are more likely to have fewer options when it comes to shopping, face more medical discrimination based on their weight, and even be paid less than their skinny counterparts.

By ignoring these facts and focusing on how our feelings

feed into body image, we allow inequality to run rife, while capitalism continues to cash in on whichever body type they decide to place on a pedestal that year. Advertising campaigns, magazine covers and marginal marketing shifts in weight-loss brands do not do anything to meaningfully improve the lives of fat people, nor do they shift societal attitudes towards obesity and bodily differences. Instead, we exist within a juxtaposition in which the general population believe they are accepting of everyone no matter their shape or size, but still continue to enforce fatphobia, racism, ableism and transphobia in their everyday lives.

There is a difference between feeling ostracised by advertising and facing actual discrimination on a daily basis. However, people who are conventionally attractive don't conjure up confidence issues from thin air. Fat people, people of colour, gender-non-conforming people and disabled people face tangible structural inequality with regards to their appearance. But anyone who grows up conditioned as a woman will experience aesthetic-based discrimination based on their gender and how they look. Even the most attractive women in the world are belittled based on aesthetics. We aren't born hating ourselves. For our entire modern history, women's bodies have existed in patriarchal society for the sole purpose of being judged. We're viewed as objects that can be debated, tweaked and altered based on the whim of men who dictate desirability to the masses.

You're hated for being too big, resented for being too small and ridiculed either way. The focus on optimising the way we look is presented as the *raison d'être* of the female experience, and we're expected to dedicate our lives to tips and tricks that will keep us in the prime of our youth for as long as possible. Even if you're not fat, society finds a way to convince you that you are, with the demonisation of carrying a few extra pounds being the reason I spent my teenage years utterly miserable in my own body.

The universality of self-loathing is the reason why the allure of body positivity is so potent. We all – regardless of what type of body we possess – deserve to feel good about ourselves. But beauty standards won't magically disappear through self-affirmations and good intentions. Without dismantling fatphobia, being bigger will always exist as a fear that wriggles its way into skinny people's minds. The focus by the movement on embracing our individual bodies ignores all the reasons why we hate them in the first place: because we've always been told that if you're not skinny, you're unworthy of love or attention.

These thoughts will always exist in our minds in some subconscious way unless they are dismantled at the source. We need to view self-worth and beauty on a societal level that accepts our bodily liberation as connected with all different intersections of identity – and not just based on how we individually feel when we look in the mirror. The tension between the fact that we all feel bad ourselves but are told we shouldn't is because body positivity is faulty, and peddled by the very people who sought to oppress us in the first place, not because there is anything wrong with any single one of us.

The movement's close ties to capitalism through marketing, branding and advertising are a modern development. Traditionally, advertising has been the beating heart of our bodily displeasure, not the battleground for our collective liberation. Diet culture seeks to control, largely targeting women to profit from our insecurities. While all women born in the last century feel the effects of this industry, the beginnings of our obsession with food restriction were far more targeted. Long before SlimFast existed, colonists dating as far back as the eighteenth century pioneered fatphobia as a tool to separate people of colour from whiteness. Initially tying Black people to an inherent obesity stemming from a lack of control, scientists went on throughout the nineteenth century to blame health disparities between races on cultural differences such as poor diet, and, again, a lack of self-control within Black and Latin communities.

The ability to restrict your diet and rationalise your relationship with food became synonymous with whiteness, a way of thinking first introduced by the ancient Greeks and then the Romans, whose belief system was laced with ideas stressing the importance of moderation and balance. While fatphobia may have started as a moral and civil issue, these ideologies have endured across modern history and become central to our health system and the way we view our bodies. Overt racism has paved the way for not only our current fatphobic landscape, but medical bias against the Black community and fat people right up to the present day.

Dieting is big business, with the current UK industry worth two billion a year. As much as these companies tell us they want us to love ourselves, their entire business model is reliant on ensuring we don't. The body positivity movement is irrevocably tied to companies that tell us we can buy our way out of the same insecurities they rely on for income. While our predecessors fought these corporations and the ideas they peddled head on, we now place them on a pedestal. Where fat acceptance activists actively fought to reject the ideas pushed by weight-loss corporations, we are now happy to accept their shift towards 'wellness' as signalling the end of systemic weight-based bias.

Every time a bigger woman is offered a contract with a food supplement company, clothing brand or feminine hygiene product, we applaud it as a win, when really we should be questioning why these companies hold so much power over us in the first place. If self-love really does come from within, then the only successful way to liberate ourselves from fatphobia is to cut our ties with capitalism as much as we can. While fat liberation has never been as explicitly co-opted by advertising as it is now, companies' newly found moral compass didn't appear from thin air. Before we looked towards corporations to do the right thing, activists were forging the path for body positivity right up to the early days of Instagram. These ideas were then taken up by the advertising industry, who saw a threatening shift in how women felt about themselves and an urgency to provide campaigns that catered to a new era of women who sought to reject diet culture.

Watching the female figures in our lives constantly restricting what they ate in order to look a certain way, our generation began to break away from the framework that dictated that women must avoid indulgence at all cost. This left the diet industry scrambling for a way to sell us products that didn't rely on the urge to shrink ourselves. Their interest in wellness, representation and inclusivity has seldom been genuine, but rather a strategic reaction to changing perceptions of how we view our bodies. We need to untangle the mindset that we should yearn for representation from those who do not care about us, and remove the power from industries that are only willing to afford us the bare minimum.

Even with this push to be accepting and understanding, the body positivity movement's messaging around fatness is less welcoming. More often than not fat people are told to strive for acceptance rather than love; that if we're not being oppressed and harassed, that should be enough and we should be grateful. The popularised imagery around body positivity falls into line with the idea of acceptance: rolls, stretch marks, spots and other blemishes are on display under garish lighting for all to see. 'Diverse' campaigns more often than not dress fat bodies in unflattering nude underwear that highlights their differences from the ones that walk down catwalks.

Rarely do you see a fat woman portraying glamour. Nor are you likely to find imagery depicting fatness as beautiful in and of itself, as opposed to trying to prove a point that correlating fatness with beauty is a novelty rather than the norm. The work of those seeking more than simply tolerance for their bodies in our society has been pushed aside for a body-positive agenda that prioritises assimilation into capitalism over true radical change. Ultimately, we're just looking at the world through a new lens, while upholding the same beauty standards that have existed since the dawn of time.

Self-love has been peddled to us as a final destination: that if we behave in the right way, and buy the right things, we can live a happy life and find inner peace with our appearance. That one day, society will catch up and stop tokenising those who look different in order to appear progressive. In reality, how we view ourselves will always fluctuate, regardless of body size or proximity to conventional beauty. In the same moment that I adore myself, I can catch how I look at the wrong angle and immediately swing into self-hatred for hours on end. But for body positivity to work, we all need to individually de-centre ourselves from the conversation. Our beauty and perception of what makes a good body have been defined by people the rules will never truly affect. Our ability to love ourselves will never be down to individual choice or a lifetime spent worrying over how we appear to others. Instead, we need a complete overhaul regarding who controls our idea of beauty in the first place.

When it comes to my own appearance, on a good day I view my fatness as something to be proud of. Being fat means enjoying the things I like, ignoring the views of the people I don't, and accepting that my beauty is not reliant on the way I live my life. It means ignoring a world that continuously tells me to change, listening to my own body, and trusting that living with a few stomach rolls is far better than lying in a hospital bed due to my digestive system depriving itself of the things it needs. I could spin my body shape as a radical rally against restrictive beauty standards and capitalism, but ultimately this is the happiest way for me to live – both in body and in mind.

Of course there are still days where I pull at the parts of me that stick out; I poke my stomach and stare at my deep stretch marks for hours, secretly hoping that something will change and I'll wake up skinny. I spend hours on other people's social media wishing I had their confidence, bone structure or body shape. But ultimately I'm not willing to sacrifice my health or the things I enjoy doing to see my ribcage once again. I would much rather we all work to change our attitudes towards fatness than alter my figure to abide by a damaging status quo. In 'More People Should Be FAT', Llewellyn Louderback writes, 'inside millions of thin Americans are fat men and women'. I want to live in a world in which we stop romanticising the ability to restrict ourselves of the things we love, and instead embrace who we really are – no matter where that puts us on the BMI scale. For now, I try my hardest to remember that being fat is no bad thing, because once upon a time, it saved my life.

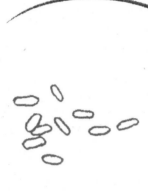

The hospital

The assumption that modern medicine is built on equality is a lie.

In hospital, you are nothing but a body — trying to control how that body is treated when all of the pain incurred is necessary to get answers is a futile process. Disabled people are surveilled under medicine for their entire lives.

'You're too young to be here' at first sounds like a compli-
ment. Nothing matches the rush of being asked to present
your ID when buying a bottle of Prosecco, or the flood of
serotonin when someone compliments your youthful glow.
But when hearing the words constantly echoed at you from
the side of a hospital bed, it can feel like a curse. Our tendency to clamour at any opportunity to be called young is
because youth connotes a certain type of freedom; you're
seen as the most hot you'll ever be, and harnessing the most
potential you'll ever have in your life. I've been told I was too
young to be constantly in contact with the NHS ever since
my first fateful stay in the acute medical ward at age nineteen.

Since then, I have visited the hospital countless times.
I have had six colonoscopies, one endoscopy, two MRI
scans, transit studies, many X-rays, more than seventy-five
injections of immunosuppressants, countless blood tests,
hundreds of consultation appointments, a handful of trips
to A&E and more medication changes than I can count.
Most people hate hospitals, and for good reason: the deaths
of loved ones, terrible news and pain all occur within their
walls. But over time, their emotional hold begins to fade, as
being hit with medical revelation after medical revelation
becomes as common as contracting a cold.

There are only so many times you can panic about receiving a blood test, squirm as a blood pressure cuff wraps around your arm, cutting off your circulation, or cry in a consultant's office. Living my life in and out of medical institutions has become as much a part of my normality as going to the supermarket or having a haircut. However, there are still small things that feel like being stabbed in the heart; that send me into a spiral of self-pity and serve as a bleak reminder of the unfairness of it all. 'You're too young to be here' may seem innocuous, and is almost certainly never meant to make me feel bad about myself. But these words, intended as comfort, in fact provide the exact opposite. They remind me that while others enjoy their lives, I am stuck in a limbo of taking medicine, attending procedures and searching for answers.

There's a misconception that diagnosis provides clarity; that once there is an actual clinical acknowledgement of what is going on inside your body, what follows is a clear path to getting better, or at least to normality. The reality is more murky, complicated, and at times, infuriating. Navigating the NHS can often feel like playing the most long-winded game of snakes and ladders in the world. If your condition isn't linear in terms of diagnosis leading to treatment, which then results in recovery, you're often left in the endless maze of our healthcare system, with professionals who struggle to make sense of your symptoms and what they mean. As the number of years I've lived with chronic illness begin to catch up with the ones in which I was well, I find myself feeling less and less sure about the inner workings of my body. After being passed around different specialists, all poking, prodding, and investigating various parts of me, I feel no more at peace with my conditions and what they mean.

We all intrinsically believe that our doctors and medical professionals are there to do us good, and that medicine can solve most – if not all – of our problems, be it a broken leg or a sadness that just won't shift. For many who use the NHS as a short-term service solving short-term health problems, this is the case. Criticising our healthcare feels icky; it's free, overstretched and underfunded. I've spent enough hours researching 'how much does it cost a person with Crohn's disease to live in America?' to know that in many other countries, I wouldn't be cared for at all. But all the good that our national health service enacts does not erase the difficulty chronically ill and disabled people experience when seeking proper long-term management of their conditions. Problems that only increase tenfold if your identity intersects with femininity, race, gender nonconformity or any other marginalisation under the sun.

The reason why people with chronic illnesses and multiple diagnoses find it so hard to seek meaningful help and relief via our public medical systems is not necessarily because the answers don't exist. While it is true that many chronic conditions and their treatments suffer from a lack of understanding and research, this lack of knowledge is in part due to the history of medicine diminishing the experiences of women, people of colour, trans people and gender-non-conforming people – dismissing their pain and rendering it unimportant. The assumption that modern medicine is built on equality is a lie. In actuality, the foundations of medicine, healthcare and science are steeped in philosophical values that seek to create inequality, not reduce or solve it.

Patriarchal white supremacist Western society has always used medicine and science as a vessel to legitimise its own biases and prejudices. Tracing all the way back to the ancient Greeks, philosophers such as Aristotle began to build the roadmap for medical sexism that would persevere right up to the present day. Along with other 'great thinkers' of the time, he labelled women as 'mutilated males', declaring them colder and weaker than men, thus incapable of warming their blood and purifying their souls; leading to the belief that men were active while women were lazy. The idea that we still give so much power to the thoughts of philosophers who have been dead for multiple centuries seems ludicrous.

But while our current science-based healthcare system may not overtly declare that cisgender women have biological differences that mean they are inferior to cisgender men, the history of medicine dictates that science has nearly always been used as a tool to oppress women rather than liberate them. Modern medicine was built on the desire to separate women from men and secure women's place as subordinate in society. The intellectual seed, planted by the ancient Greeks, that asserted that women were biologically inferior to men was carried through to medieval thinking that led to the first instances of modern medicine, creating a backbone for centuries of medical bias that is yet to be broken.

Early sketches of female skeletons, published in the eighteenth century, depicted women with small heads, a petite build and wide pelvises. These were not accurate anatomical depictions, but rather artistic renditions – and images that became highly contested among the scientific community in relation to which most closely represented reality. Pelvises were drawn large to prove that women's only purpose on earth was to rear children, and the smaller heads were intended to provide evidence that women were intellectually inferior to their male counterparts. The emerging interest in tracing the biological make-up of women was no coincidence.

At a time at which great advances were being made in the development of government, science, education and more, men were looking for a reason to keep women out of the equation. They turned to science to reaffirm the fact that women were not fit for public life, or for any form of power and responsibility beyond housekeeping.

Male bodies became the blueprint against which women's anatomy was judged; from the outset, women were not considered different yet equal. Instead, scientists became obsessed with asserting the superiority of male bodies by pointing out the 'flaws' in female ones. Though wishing to distance science from femininity, those working in the field became obsessed with it.

Their enduring quest to oppress women resulted in the construction of the gender binary in Western medicine. This hatred of femininity cemented our black-and-white thinking when it comes to the rigidity of gender, and has ensured that medicine will always be dogged by seemingly immovable definitions of 'manhood' and 'womanhood'. Multiple textbooks and studies were published solely dedicated to tracing the differences between men and women. These scientific 'revelations' penetrated society, held women back and justified their oppression, with their contribution to society limited by their bodies' ability to bear children, while men were considered intellectual due to the vastness of their minds.

But these depictions – drawn before a time in which we could accurately study the human body – did not only stem from a scientific sexism that wished to put men ahead. They were also intended to represent the most beautiful and naturally perfect version of femininity, despite the fact that they were literally representing nothing more than a bunch of bones. From the beginning, science has been used to rationalise treating women as lesser beings, and has valued beauty over accuracy in order to assert the fact that we should value women based on how beautiful they are to the male eye.

This historical sexism doesn't only affect cisgender women seeking refuge in our medical systems. The fact that patriarchal clinicians hated women enough to make us practically subhuman has a lasting impact on transgender and non-binary people who aim to seek supportive, understanding healthcare in our modern society. With more than 13,500 trans and non-binary people on the waiting list for NHS gender-identity clinics, and the average waiting time stretching to eighteen months, medicine's desire to disregard anyone who doesn't conform to gender stereotypes that are outdated by centuries is preventing many people from living happy and full lives.

In modern contexts, we view health as the great equaliser. We believe that biases from the past have dissipated in favour of quantitative evidence and scientific fact. No matter your wealth status, gender, race, age or body type, sickness is thought to not discriminate, with the assumption that we all receive the same care once it does strike. What differs, however, is the treatment we receive depending on the intersections of our identity and proximity to societal marginalisation. It has been found that an algorithm widely used in US hospitals systematically discriminates against

Black patients, and does not refer them to programmes to aid their recovery at the same rate as it does for equally unwell white people.

A 2016 study concluded that nearly half of first- and second-year medical students believed that Black people have thicker skin and experience less pain than white people, while another paper found that Black people were 40 per cent less likely to be prescribed pain medication. Fatness and body image also impact how you are treated by medical professions. Fat patients are more likely to be discriminated against by doctors, with any and all of their health problems being ascribed to their weight with no scientific evidence to support these claims. Essentially, if you aren't a cisgender white man, you're going to struggle when trying to seek unbiased medical help.

During my hospital visits, I have experienced nurses refusing me my contraceptive medicine as they were heavily religious, my boyfriend being barred from visiting in case we had sex in my room, and a doctor repeatedly, and creepily, calling me a 'good girl' during an internal vaginal ultrasound. I have also been denied gynaecological examinations when experiencing pain, and been refused a check of my contraceptive IUD, only to find out five years later that it had been in the wrong place, and therefore was not only ineffective, but painful too. But medical sexism runs deeper than casually misogynist encounters that leave patients feeling at best unsettled and at worst violated, with their serious undiagnosed or misdiagnosed health problems ignored.

I've heard stories of female medical students and nurses witnessing senior male staff commenting on the desirability of female patients while they were under sedation, with complaints to HR ignored and female members of staff shifted around different hospitals to bury stories of misconduct. These types of behaviours do not just impact how the patient feels emotionally about their visits to the hospital or reduce the trust they have in medical staff. Sexist encounters signal a cohort of medical professionals who view women as objects and subordinates rather than equals or even people.

Studies have found that male clinicians are more likely to call female patients 'girls' rather than 'women'. While this small linguistic slip-up may seem minor, it reinforces the fact that in a medical setting, women are constantly infantilised, associating us with vulnerability and a dependency on men to make the right decisions for us. When female staff found themselves making the same mistake, they almost always corrected themselves. Male doctors rarely did.

While my subsequent experiences with healthcare have been far from simple or positive, initially finding out I had Crohn's disease was a pretty straightforward, yet slightly traumatic blur. As my myriad of experiences with chronic illnesses pile up, my memories of those first few days are hard to grasp, but what I do remember is that being diagnosed initially felt like a solution rather than the beginning of many, many more problems. After experiencing symptoms for around six months, I was referred by my GP to the hospital. From there, I was rushed from my first specialist gastroenterology appointment into a surgical procedure after the clinician realised I was much more seriously unwell than I'd ever thought possible.

Following that, I lay drugged up in A&E for hours while they decided where to put me. Finally I was placed on a ward surrounded by people experiencing what seemed like the last moments of their lives, with screams echoing around the room. Disorientated, unwell and feeling the anaesthetic disappear from my system, I began to panic – and refused to stay unless I was moved to a more private environment. When finally presented with my own room (which I was only given due to the fact that I was experiencing chronic diarrhoea and not because of my slightly brattish outburst), I was hooked up to a drip and left alone aside from the regular monitoring of my blood pressure and other vitals.

For the first twenty-four hours, I had no idea what liquid medicine they were running straight into my veins. Explanations were rushed as doctors and nurses did their rounds, and a part of me refused to absorb any information, as to understand what was going on would mean accepting that I would be unwell for my entire life. I had no choice but to put my absolute trust in the hands of the staff who were caring for me, despite the fact that I didn't feel any different to how I had felt for the months leading up to that moment. I was insistent on clawing back any semblance of control I could retain over the situation: from trying to force doctors and nurses to share every tiny detail of my treatment with me, to discharging myself temporarily for walks, insisting on visitors and generally believing I could think and talk my way out of chronic illness through strong will and a bossiness I'd been told to play down my entire life.

By the second day, I'd had enough, and declared I would rather kill myself than spend any more time in a room with no answers, being barred from seeing my loved ones. The thought of being alone in hospital, not knowing what my future would hold, was perhaps the worst thing that could ever happen to nineteen-year-old me. What I wanted was to be able to do things my way, for everyone around me to stop panicking, for all of these sudden new-found problems to disappear, and to stop being treated as though I had very little autonomy or didn't understand what was happening due to my age.

Despite the fact that my outburst was quite obviously a moment of desperation from an extremely dramatic young woman, in rushed the mental-health crisis team – followed by a diagnosis of anxiety and depression. I have definitely always been anxious and depressed. I spent most of my teenage years in tears and began suffering full-blown panic attacks in the months leading up to my first hospitalisation. In the years following diagnosis, I have been on and off antidepressants and in and out of therapy. Overall, I would describe myself as a fairly stable mentally unstable person.

Since that first fateful stay, I've found that the only way to keep relatively sane during my periods of time in hospital is to disassociate. I've had to accept I will never be in control of my body, that flare-ups of my symptoms can occur out of the blue, and that the pain experienced both inside and outside of medical institutions is unavoidable. Being chronically ill, for me, means constantly walking the line between advocating for myself and accepting there are some things I cannot change. My fear of needles, once non-existent, now bubbles under the surface each time I experience a vein bursting during a cannula fitting, or after hours of sitting in a chair with a phlebotomy nurse unable to locate a vein for my blood test. The fact that my treatment and various medications have put me more at risk of terminal illness further down the line has to be ignored.

My hesitancy about being touched by strangers or speaking openly about how often I go to the toilet and what that looks and feels like has no choice but to be entirely disregarded. In the hospital, you are nothing but a body; trying to control how that body is treated when all the pain incurred is necessary to get answers is a futile process.

Disabled people are medically surveilled for their entire lives. The only tool I have found to cope with invasive questions, treatments and procedures is to entirely disconnect from my physicality and allow the waves of pain, anxiety and insecurity to wash over me as much as possible. To leave any semblance of my personality and thoughts at the door and succumb to being a vessel for treatment.

On the flip side, chronically ill people – myself included – are so often left with the burden of pushing for answers, chasing phone calls and booking appointments that dissociation only gets you so far. Being chronically ill is like having the most depressing and time-consuming side-hustle in the world. Even when I do successfully manage to swallow down the feelings of existential dread during treatment, each painful moment comes flooding back in the days and weeks following my medical encounters. From the nurse who tried to comfort me as I burst into tears in a recovery room by telling me that *of course* I should be expected to feel suicidal while living with such a horrible disease, and that learning to love myself would be the answer to all my problems, to the many medical practitioners who have said I should simply destress if I wish to solve my health issues – as if having multiple invasive treatments to determine what is going on in my body isn't stressful in and of itself.

To minimise this post-hospital anxiety, I have managed to separate my life somewhat into two halves: in medical treatment, and out of it. Months and months go by in which I can ignore the hospital and just live with the aches, pains and unpredictability of my symptoms quietly and alone. But those periods of time in which I do find myself in medical care consume my life. I have to keep a strict schedule of when to call the doctors, when to follow up, how often to plead with clinicians and when to push back on their assessments in an exhausting game of tug of war that is never-ending. I have to frequently weigh up whether I want to try a medication with a myriad of side effects or to just make do with my health as it is. I am constantly debating with myself whether to ignore my body in order to not cause too much disruption in my day-to-day life, or to seek medical health and be set back on the same path of appointments, examinations and treatments that rarely leave me more well than when I started.

While I don't think my experiences with depression and anxiety can be attributed to living with chronic illness, the two intersect. Rates of depression are higher in those who have Crohn's disease than in the general population, with the unpredictable nature of the illness being blamed for stress, hopelessness and extreme sadness. Though logically it makes absolute sense that those who have conditions that can limit their experiences deal with serious bouts of depression and anxiety, the mental health of marginalised, chronically ill and disabled people is often weaponised in order to discredit the seriousness of their condition.

Women's mental well-being has been conflated with their physical health since the early days of medicine, with science declaring men to be level-headed, scientific beings and women emotional child-bearers. This feminisation of feeling changed how women were treated medically, with seventeenth- and eighteenth-century scientists believing that in order to cure the physical ailments of women, psychology must be central to their treatment. Medical papers of the time tied the emotional with the physical, reporting that many women's bodily health issues stemmed from being emotionally unsettled, due to not leading the appropriate domestic lifestyle that their biology dictated.

Even before the invention of modern medicine, philosophy historically used our bodies to deem women deviants. Democritus declared the uterus to be the cause of a thousand sicknesses, with other philosophers believing that those with uteruses suffered each illness twice over due to having one. Plato argued that uteruses were animals independent from the rest of the body that held their own ability to move, and both Vesalius and Galen wrote that the uterus in fact had horns sprouting from each side – thus tying anatomy to the devil. During the nineteenth century, medical researchers who believed in an unquestionable bond between the physical and the mental outlined that the only way to solve the mystery of the female psyche was to look between our legs; with gynaecologists asserting themselves as the best people to treat a woman's mental health problems, as the female mind and reproductive organs were considered one and the same.

With scientists using biology to dictate men as reasoned and superior and women as emotional and inferior, the fact that those presenting with physical symptoms were often distressed about their illnesses was used to declare women mentally disturbed. Clinicians used this rationale to treat conditions such as hysteria, an ailment thought to affect women more than men due to our irritability and general bad temperament. Initially, hysteria was thought to stem from a deviance in the womb. Though many of the symptoms were physical and wide-ranging – chest pain, stomach cramps, high or low temperature, high or low blood pressure, loss of appetite and more – eventually, in the nineteenth century, hysteria was deemed a psychological disorder relating to uncontrollable emotion, and treated as such.

Women were institutionalised, and treatments included doctors performing sexual acts on patients in their care, pregnancy, and the application of oils on the female genitals, among other generally repulsive, non-scientific 'cures'. This type of treatment stems from a desire to control women over any actual proof-based merit. Rather than seeking out the intricacies of each patient's issues, women were lumped together under the umbrella of uncontrollable madness. Historically, whether by ancient philosophers or anatomical artists, womanly evil can be found both in our

DNA and in our minds. The suppression of our thoughts and feelings through seemingly scientific means has proven itself time and time again to be little more than an attempt to ensure marginalised people are not taken seriously.

The idea that the vibrator was invented by doctors to cure hysteria is history, but the assumption that women are overemotional and not fit to accurately describe the inner workings of their own bodies still persists today. Research has found that clinicians often specifically take issue with female patients who refuse to accept that medicine can do nothing more to help them and continue to seek help after the point at which medical staff believe all options to be exhausted. These same clinicians view women as failures, due to the fact that they have, in their eyes, not done enough to look after themselves and prevent what has happened to them.

Doctors have also been found to resent women who do their own research, trust their own feelings in regard to their bodies, and continue to seek answers once a specialist has turned them away. In these cases, medical staff are likely to refer the patient to psychological treatment – therefore further perpetuating the stereotype of an unwell woman being crazy, illogical and over the top.

Despite history, the idea that our mental health can be linked to our physical ailments doesn't necessarily have to be negative. Of course, if you are unwell, you are more stressed, and increasingly likely to be unhappy. Being more attuned, from a clinician's point of view, to what might be going on under the skin of patients who present as on edge would probably lead to better understanding between patient and doctor, a more streamlined diagnostic process, and a patient experience that isn't triggering to the point of having to emotionally detach yourself from your body. However, instead of building a holistic approach to mental and physical health, the stereotype that women are hysterical beings prone to overreaction is still rife in our medical systems.

Considering that so much of medical diagnosis relies on the relaying of how things feel from patient to doctor, the fact that we are so often not believed leaves thousands of marginalised people in limbo. Studies have found that those who consistently require medical attention actually see a decrease in the quality of their care, as they are viewed by both society and doctors as already damaged, with little that can be done to help. At this point, I have spent so much of my adult life in and out of doctor's offices that my body belongs as much to the hospital that holds my medical records as it does to me. I will always be viewed as damaged because of my conditions, whether through the lens of sadness due to the unfairness of my position considering my youth, or simply because I will never be well.

Though I have had various diagnoses throughout my time as a sick girl (inflammatory bowel disease being the big one, though I also have IBS, polycystic ovary syndrome, a hiatal hernia, a sensitive gut, and more), none of these labels, so far, has practically improved my life. They only contribute to the confusion I feel about my body and who I am. The times when I have to relay something as abstract as pain to complete strangers do not make me feel more confident about asserting myself in medical situations. In fact, constantly being pointed to a numerical scale and being asked to attribute the constant churning and curdling in my stomach to a cold, definite symbol has caused the opposite.

I am constantly gaslighting myself. I berate myself for being stupid and causing a fuss each time I call my specialist. Once those calls have ended, I spend hours replaying the conversation in my head and rebuking myself after limply taking 'no' for an answer when requesting further help with the symptoms that hold me back from living a relatively normal life. With each cab fare I spend ferrying myself to and from appointments, I question what the point of it all is, and whether life would be easier if I just gave up trying to get better.

While experiencing long periods of relative wellness between the times in which I am completely and horribly riddled with illness, I wonder whether I am sick at all. Whether it's all in my head and it's actually my distorted mind that is causing me to put myself through further harm in an elaborate ruse to make my life harder. Stuck with no concrete answers as to why we feel the way we do and distrusting of our medical institutions, it's no wonder so many of us see any eventual acknowledgement via diagnosis or treatment as validation of our lived experiences. When people have to fight so hard for something, it makes sense that once we actually get it, we feel as though the hardest battle has been won. But the reality of living with long-term incurable illness is not as simple as having a doctor finally say they understand how we feel.

While the aforementioned sexism implies that all men working in medical fields are women-hating toads, the reality isn't so simple. Research has found that more often than not, clinicians are not calculated in their behaviour towards female patients. However, what this treatment towards women and other marginalised people signals is a subconscious reinforcement of men being experts and women being ill-informed. Most doctors, of course, do not want to harm their patients. However, covert sexism and racism penetrates our medical institutions, meaning doctors are less likely to believe women and marginalised people, offer them help or take their pain seriously.

With a scarcity of marginalised people in leadership roles, backwards ideologies that sound impossibly prehistoric still influence how medicine is practised and patients are treated today. These experiences aren't the fault of any particular practitioner or hospital. Instead, what I have been subject to during my twenties is symptomatic of a system that has never deemed women's bodies worthy of consideration. Health bias is written into our history. Like all industries, the tools by which we measure our well-being have overwhelmingly been dictated by men. Men who have conflated hysteria with life-endangering medical conditions. Men who dreamed up the first female skeletons with enlarged hips and tiny heads in order to assert their own dominance. Men who used sexual acts to 'cure' women of mental illness. We may have moved on from the more extreme medical bias demonstrated in the early days of modern medicine, but women still to this day struggle to have their pain taken seriously.

There is a long history of marginalised people's pain being treated at best with suspicion and at worst complete dismissal. The most depressing part of it all is that it feels like there is little movement in the way of positive change for those who find themselves in frequent contact with doctors, nurses and other medical staff. I can try and be the strongest version of myself, to push against doctors who dismiss me and fight as hard as I can to get the answers I need. I can also try to build a healthier relationship with medicine, somewhere closer to the middle of the spectrum, rather than either dismissing it completely or wallowing as a poor little sick girl. But I cannot change an institution.

In the UK, the NHS is in decline. After a pandemic that saw its resources pushed to the absolute limit, it is now being sold for parts to private healthcare companies in a move that only leads to a decline of quality in both long-term and short-term treatment for those who need it. To make healthcare a more inclusive and accessible place for marginalised people would require an entire societal overhaul towards actually believing them.

Although it sounds simple, we're all guilty of indulging our inner cynic when deciding on how much we really trust people to tell the truth. Our treatment of marginalised people in medical settings – both past and present – is reflective of how we view them in the wider world. And until we begin to take them seriously when they say they are hurting, no improvement can be made to the lives of people who deal with not being believed on a daily basis. With the entirety of history working against us, visiting the hospital may emotionally sting less each time I walk through the doors, but that doesn't mean I, or anyone else in my position, am any closer to the answers, treatment or understanding I deserve when tackling what goes on underneath my skin.

This too shall pass

Our immediate response to hearing that something is wrong with someone is to try and fix them.

We no longer avoid sinning in case it'll cause us to be shut out of heaven, but we do avoid unhealthy behaviour for fear it will make us sick.

Everyone around me is obsessed with the idea that one day I will magically get better. That one day I'll discover something that takes away all my problems and I'll be free to live the rest of my life as a well person. This despite the fact that they know there is no overcoming my condition, and that it is something I will never be cured of. In the early years of my diagnosis, I was equally fixated with the idea of returning to the same level of health I experienced pre-Crohn's disease. I'd honestly never even heard of chronic illness before then, and I truly thought that as long as an illness wasn't terminal, it was possible to cure it. Even when I understood that my condition would never disappear, I didn't fully realise how much my well-being would be permanently altered from that point onwards.

During that first year, when initial medication didn't bring me back to the level of health I felt before I became sick, I panicked and hastily rushed into more extreme treatment in an attempt to subdue my symptoms and the fear I was feeling. In reality, I probably needed a therapist as opposed to a constantly increasing dose of medication. On the whole, what doctors fail to communicate when presented with an incurable illness is that 'remission' does not mean 'cured'. I thought that without active disease in my body, there would be no reason why my life wouldn't ping back to just the same as it was when I was well. That if I could heal my insides, I could live peacefully for a finite amount of time.

However, eight years on from diagnosis, and having spent a large portion of that in clinical remission, I slowly but surely realised that life never goes back to 'normal' once you are chronically ill. While you may not be dying, you're unlikely to move through the world in the same way you once did. Most days I still experience pain to some degree, fatigue still has a hold over my existence, and let's not even begin with my bowel movements. Medically, my condition is considered to be somewhere between fully lethal and inactive. I'm not unwell enough to warrant serious medical intervention, but not well enough to live my life normally. This leaves me in a weird flux. Most days I feel like a fraud in my own body and am left second-guessing my symptoms.

Spending much of my time thinking about my health is unavoidable. No matter how hard I try to push reality to the back of my mind and get on with things I want to do, my illness is always there, lurking. I have, however, moved on from the idea of fixing myself outside the medication that supresses my symptoms as much as possible. I am not desperate or rich enough to try every supplement, potion or treatment peddled on the private market. Of course, I continue to follow treatment plans as closely as I can, but any lifestyle changes I have made to ease my Crohn's disease have largely been pointless. I've tried various exclusionary diets that have failed to cure my stomach pain and have only succeeded in making me depressed.

On multiple occasions I've added things to my daily routine – from flaxseed in the morning to vitamin D at night. But as I cure one deficiency, another always rears its head. I could spend my every waking moment tweaking how I live my life until something finally clicks and I am magically well, but it feels futile, unlikely to ever actually work, and also makes me miserable. Every time I try a 'wonder cure' that doesn't work, I feel like a failure. I would rather be happy with a dysfunctional body than feeling worthless while spending every waking moment trying to fix myself.

However, the idea that I don't aspire to wellness seems insane to anyone who doesn't live with illness. It's not that I enjoy being unwell; there are so many symptoms I try to banish from my body with no success. It's more that the pursuit of trying to fix myself serves as a constant reminder that my broken parts are permanent, and not something that can be absolved with a bi-annual juice cleanse.

When seeing someone in pain, it's natural to want to give them advice. Whether it's a friend going through a break-up, somebody you work with who's struggling with a task, or every single member of your friendship group chiming in with their insights as an argument kicks off in the group chat. Equally, many of us revel in receiving advice. Sometimes we ask people their opinion so we can have our own thoughts validated. On other occasions, it feels practically impossible to move forward in a situation without help from others. But well-meaning advice is not always benevolent. In some cases, suggestions from our loved ones are a subtle way to diffuse hard words we need to hear, and the upset the advice causes is necessary.

But on other occasions, these suggestions come from a place of misguidance, and can cause more harm than good. This particularly applies when giving advice on an identity you have no lived experience of, be it illness, disability, race, femininity, queerness, fatness or any other marginalisation. Over the last half-decade, I've been on the receiving end of every type of advice imaginable concerning my chronic illness. From a specific yogurt brand that my mum swears will cure my condition, and family members advising yoga for my mental instability, to empathetic Instagram mutuals sending medically unproven advice from dubious influencers. While undoubtedly those who offer up advice relating to the health of an acquaintance or loved one do not mean to cause upset, the feelings of frustration and misunderstanding that often arise when having these discussions are likely to cause more harm than good.

The most frustrating part of receiving advice from a well person when you are sick is that they assume you've never considered whichever product or treatment they're peddling. Each individual acts as though their idea will come as a revelation, rather than being advice you've already read a thousand times in the midst of a desperate flare-up-induced doom scroll. Even the small complaint of a stomach ache seems to welcome an onslaught of suggestions from people who do not understand your symptoms but are sure they have ingenious ideas about how to prevent and treat them. While not deliberate, this creates an assumption that those who experience chronic illness and disability are largely naive about the possible treatments and lifestyle changes that could help them.

For the first few years after diagnosis, nobody around me knew anything about my illness. I would have to explain the basics over and over again each time I chose to disclose that I had Crohn's disease – and sometimes I still do. Now, everyone's an expert on how to treat pain, or fatigue, or any other ailment you find yourself dealing with, even if they have never experienced it themselves. We are constantly bombarded with holistic health advice, largely via our phone screens, that calls for no further interrogation or fact-checking. The power dynamics at play between unwell and well people are not accidental, nor are they spiteful. At the end of the day, our immediate response to hearing that something is wrong with someone is to offer help.

Despite my years of advice dealing with the well-meaning but oblivious, I still find myself dishing out unwarranted tips to the people I talk to when they're telling me that they feel poorly. With the ever-expanding wellness industry working its way into every crevice of our world, both online and off, it can often seem impossible to avoid unsolicited pointers on how to manage your day-to-day existence, unwell or otherwise. But this shift towards us all being health 'experts' has darker implications than a few hurt feelings. The reality is, unwell people and their loved ones are not the only portion of the population obsessed with health.

In fact, being well has become a global fixation – one that has been slowly rumbling away in the back of our collective consciousness since the eighties. While dwindling health used to be a problem only for those who were experiencing medical problems, being as healthy as humanly possible is now of concern to us all. Not only that, but we are also expected to pre-empt any future medical emergencies by limiting the way we behave in the present. We are urged to consider our health and well-being as a determining factor in every decision we make, and are constantly looking for ways to improve our existence by optimising the way our insides operate.

Wellness, in the twenty-first century, has come to replace religion as the moral signposting by which we live our lives. We no longer avoid sinning in case it'll cause us to be shut out of heaven, but we do avoid unhealthy behaviour for fear it will make us sick. We value being physically well over practically everything else, and envelop this idea of wellness into nearly every aspect of our lives. Our mental health is now determined by how healthy our bodies are, our concentration levels are dependent on how well we look after ourselves, and the respect we give to others is contingent on whether they care about themselves enough to watch their health.

Going to the gym is now considered a personality type, with 87 per cent of Gen Z saying they exercise more than three times a week. Millennials drink alcohol less often than the generation before them, with Gen Z drinking 20 per cent less than millennials. Smoking is no longer cool, recreational drug use is for losers, and living well is the most impressive thing you can do for yourself. We view those who ignore the things that are good for them in favour of having fun and dabbling in behaviours that are bad as deviants who do not care about their own well-being. Health has shifted from a medical concern to one that has to be viewed in terms of behaviour, and our response to 'bad' behaviours has become medicalised. Stress and burnout are no longer things we consider to be produced by our environment; instead we attribute them to imbalances in our hormones, an unsettled nervous system, or our guts screaming at us to look after ourselves. Countering that, we assume all health problems can be quelled by behavioural shifts: that my Crohn's disease can be cured with yoga, that inflammation can be reduced by eating less dairy, and that fatigue can be squashed with the right bedtime routine.

Over the last century, we have seen the medicalisation of society. Much of our lives are ruled by what scholar Robert Crawford defined as healthism: a preoccupation with personal health, the achievement of well-being, and a push towards behaviours that improve our lives and health but exist outside of medical intervention. Healthism places the responsibility on the individual to determine how well they live their lives, and defines illness as an individual choice made by people who are simply uninterested in caring for themselves effectively. While this might sound like a niche thought process, these beliefs have become the dominant discourse across advertising, the media and even politicians when discussing what constitutes healthy living. The ways in which we have been urged to take our health into our own hands are covert. We aren't being told to stop enjoying ourselves; rather, that the key to living a happy life is to be well – and that contentment is impossible without good health.

This creates friction between well and unwell people. Those who exist outside of the traditional medical system but take a keen interest in what it means to be healthy feel justified in handing out advice they've read on social media or seen on the television, in the same way they might recommend a new brand of mascara. This constant discussion as to how we can be fixed empowers the well and disempowers the sick, framing those who are intent on avoiding illness as morally superior to those who aren't. This doesn't just affect how we think of chronically ill people in terms of societal stereotypes; it actually directly impacts our quality of life.

I have lost count of the number of times a concerned friend has told me to put down whatever I'm eating as it's not good for me, or I've had to politely nod as people all around me chat among themselves for hours on end about what I could do to ease my condition. At best, these conversations are patronising. But on a bad day, they are completely humiliating – they make me feel subhuman, and as if I am not worthy of good things because my body refuses to be well. Our obsession with health splits society into two distinct categories: those who succeed and those who fail. This thinking is also highly elitist – we value those who can live in the right way over those who can't or who refuse to. These values aren't only penetrating our peer circles or the online world, but how healthcare is implemented on a national and international scale too.

For as long as I can remember, there have been debates over whether smokers should be bumped down NHS waiting lists, or whether fat people should be denied care unless they make a concerted effort to lose weight. Most recently, the discussion has centred around whether those who refuse the COVID-19 vaccine deserve to be helped if they end up in hospital due to the virus. Deciding who is and who isn't worthy of being looked after is ableist and reductionist. It ignores all the human elements of someone being unwell and reduces them to a statistic who has made a bad decision. By viewing health and disease prevention as something we all can and should partake in, we are marking many normal behaviours as unacceptable in our new healthist society.

Before healthism, many people might have silently judged those who didn't eat well, who barely exercised or who smoked. Now, it is openly acceptable to berate people for acting in a way you don't believe in. Of course, this doesn't eradicate the 'unacceptable' behaviour entirely – many healthy people continue to partake in things that are bad for them. However, these acts are either hidden from the world or discussed within the language of guilt. Eating junk food, for example, is only acceptable on a 'cheat day', or if rationalised by multiple tweets expressing regret for slipping up. Drinking too much every now and then is either followed by a giant onslaught of self-shaming via Instagram stories, or a healthy brunch snap that absolves you of all your sins and the liver of all its toxins.

Any nuance surrounding what is good for us and what is bad has been flattened. Letting off steam on a Friday night is only marginally acceptable if it's followed by a Saturday-morning trip to the gym. Eating cake to cheer yourself up is no longer a frivolous but joyful act, but instead a red flag pointing towards comfort eating and more serious problems with food down the line. We no longer only view obviously terrible things as unhealthy; anything that doesn't actively promote good health is considered a waste of time.

This juxtaposition of accepting the good and feeling utterly shameful for indulging in the bad would be fine if we viewed these behaviours as part of the balance of life, and accepted that no one can live free of sin. In moderate amounts, bad things aren't bad for us at all. There is a reason we like eating shit food and spending our weekends borderline binge-drinking – it's fun. But instead of accepting that none of us can be good all of the time, we find ways to absolve ourselves of unhealthy behaviour in order to not tarnish our reputations as visions of wellness. Not only is this way of living tedious, it's futile. By pretending that being healthy every moment of the day is the answer to happiness, we live in a way that is ruled by punishment while denying ourselves any reward.

Every time we are told that a change in our diet can prevent cancer, that certain exercises release neurochemicals that make us happier, or that a particular supplement can ward off serious disease, we are slowly but surely shifting our mindset on what constitutes health from a collective one to the plight of individuals. Health-related advice that is given by anyone but a medical professional operates on the assumption that we can work our way out of any problem we find ourselves in. That living your life in the 'right' healthy way is the answer to all your problems, and will guarantee you a long and carefree life. This thinking is enforced by the rise of our current wellness industry, which has led an entire generation of women to believe you can self-improve out of any given crisis.

Whether it's Marie Kondo convincing us that a tidy-up of our bedrooms can soothe our souls, or Gwyneth Paltrow suggesting we steam our vaginas to cure period pain, if there's something bothering you, there's someone suggesting a quick fix. On the surface, it feels hard to criticise our cultural obsession with health. Surely the fact that we're all intent on taking care of ourselves has to be a good thing. But this shift in how we view our well-being as individuals is actually extremely unhealthy. We are enabling entire swathes of people to believe themselves to be experts about their own bodies, without any of the actual scientific research required to back up such a claim.

We applaud the people who soak up the pseudo-medical advice we read online about what to eat, and idolise the individuals who organise their lives around the pursuit of wellness. But while eating more vegetables or having a tidy bedroom won't ruin your life, these small shifts in what we consider to be normal rhetoric surrounding health leave room for damaging misinformation to infiltrate our minds and penetrate our understanding of what wellness really is. Each day I see posts that link mental well-being to a treatment or lifestyle change that promises to overhaul your life. Many of these are presented without sources, from 'experts' with no actual accreditation in medicine, no formal nutritional education, or even a fitness training certificate.

Their calls to action are often easy and mindless to follow: buy a supplement, stretch in a particular way, or fork out for a treatment that will promote a niche part of your body to start working more effectively. But their intent is often not as wholesome as the posts would have you believe. By allowing them to hook you in with simple advice, you open the door to these figures to sell you a dream that not only doesn't work, but could actually be dangerous.

One extreme example of how the cult of wellness can ruin people's lives is the case of Belle Gibson. Belle rose to fame as an influencer who was battling multiple cancer diagnoses. Amassing over 300,000 Instagram followers, she claimed to have rejected traditional medicine in favour of holistic techniques and alternative therapies. But Belle wasn't simply documenting her road to recovery for her audience to observe. She built an entire brand, the Whole Pantry, with the aim of engaging other people with cancer in the same methods she was using to subdue hers. The Whole Pantry became a phenomenon, amassing 200,000 downloads within its first month on the app store, and being voted Apple's best food and drink app of 2013. From that, Belle received a book deal, resulting in a cookbook published in 2015, which helped the Whole Pantry to make over one million dollars in sales.

The problem was, none of it worked and none of it was real. Belle had never had cancer; she had invented the story in order to make a quick buck from one of the most vulnerable online communities in the world. Her hundreds of thousands of followers had been blindly following a con artist, and risking their health as they shunned modern medicine in favour of a diet consisting of only raw and natural foods. Eventually she was exposed. But retrospectively admitting her mistakes did nothing for the many people who lost control over their lives while following her advice.

Our current fixation with wellness is not only largely built on a foundation of promises that rarely deliver, it also leaves millions of people extremely vulnerable to partaking in behaviours that could leave them broke and extremely unwell. Not only that, but health becomes a middle-class pursuit rather than a universal concern. A push towards individualist health means rich people can buy Pelotons for their living rooms, while working-class people are watching their green spaces being built on, their homes being wrapped in flammable cladding and affordable, healthy food being increasingly more difficult to come by. Traditionally, working-class political plights that intersect with health have been focused on community, such as pushing for the abolition of child labour, equal provisions across communities and universal, unbiased healthcare. Conversely, middle-class people are more naturally predisposed to viewing their success as something they manifested entirely alone.

If you have more spare time, you're more likely to be able to visit holistic practitioners. If you have disposable income, trying something that may not work isn't a big deal – it wouldn't be the end of the world if an obscure treatment costing hundreds of pounds ended up being entirely pointless. Our modern pursuit of wellness only works for the people who are more likely to be able to access the resources that will help them thrive in the first place. In reality, many middle-class people are probably trying to fill the void of meaningless existence with a series of tasks that help them convince themselves they are leading active lives. If you don't have to worry about working a twelve-hour shift, if your home is safe and you don't have to worry about how you'll pay your rent, your mind is likely to wander towards issues more obscure.

When the concept of healthism was first coined by Robert Crawford, he outlined the increasing obsession with controlling your body as a response to the disappointment and lack of change following the politically charged decades of the sixties and seventies. Following on from decades of campaigning with little structural change, people turned inwards and focused on what they could do to self-improve. His theory is just as relevant today, particularly as we find ourselves living through a pandemic which leaves us completely and utterly out of control regarding our own health. During lockdowns, not only was our health in limbo, but we were faced with uncertainty in the workplace and either loneliness or turmoil in our relationships.

The only things we could control were what we ate and how we spent our one-hour allotted time slot of outdoor exercise. It makes absolute sense that wellness would worm its way into our brains with an intensity that hasn't been matched before. Our politicians have also capitalised on this new-found nervousness towards well-being, replacing collective responsibility with individual failings in their rationalisations of why coronavirus was impossible to control. Despite the fact that seizing control can feel like a positive life shift, advocating for an individualist approach to health completely strips the concept of wellness of any of the political force required to actually make life easier for those who need it.

Individualism lulls us into a false sense of security that coping on a personal level is enough, and allows us to ignore the bigger structural issues at play that keep all of us unhealthy to some degree. Healthism reroutes discontent and judgement away from our health services and governments, which can actually enact change, and towards people who do not behave in a way we find agreeable. It ignores the power structures that uphold why illness is more pervasive in some communities compared to others, and attempts to place us all on an equal playing field in which it is up to us to figure out what works and what doesn't. Essentially, it operates as a giant diversion that allows those in power to mistreat their communities and relabel oppression as laziness.

I could spend my time hunting down every possible cure and passing out huge portions of my pay to anyone who promises to make all my pain go away. I could try every single diet until one sticks, work my way through an entire medicine cabinet of supplements and not settle until my problems begin to dissipate – but in all honesty, there are more fulfilling ways for me to spend my days. In my mind, being well will never mean being totally healthy. So instead of becoming obsessed with futile attempts to delay the inevitable, I have restructured my brain in order to not feel like a sickly little toad for the rest of my life. My concept of practising wellness consists of working with what health I do have to build a life that makes me happy – even if that happiness comes from behaviours that society deems to be deviant.

The problem is, I can try and convince the world I am not totally miserable until I'm blue in the face, but health-ism has ensured that happiness is positioned as something that can only be achieved through never being sick. You can only be successful in your job, relationship, friendships and yourself if you have balanced all the spinning plates of existence with potions and practices that ensure we are

100 per cent well. It pushes the bar of existence upwards from survival and towards an expectation of complete and total happiness, which can only be achieved through living your life in the 'correct' way.

Many people, of multiple intersecting groups, can only take on the tasks and bodily needs that ensure they survive. There is no working up from just being OK, since OK will be, for me, the best it will ever get. But just because I am unwell and unable to perform health to the standard that modern life requires, it should not be assumed that I am automatically unhappy. In actuality, I would be much happier if my existence wasn't constantly regarded as something that actively works against our current belief systems. By placing responsibility on each individual person to ensure they stay well, you create pariahs of the millions of people who have no choice in the matter.

But if living as a pariah means I don't have to pretend green juice is delicious or enemas aren't awful, and can enjoy the small pleasures that stimulate endless guilt in others, I'm fine with it. The twisted correlation between health and happiness is only growing in popularity, meaning that until we re-evaluate our obsession with being well, in the eyes of the world I will always be a failure. For as long as our fixation with health optimisation continues, I exist between two extremes: being judged and content, or miserable and relatively healthy. But while others scramble to swallow false promises, under the guise that they will never be unwell, accepting reality rather than trying to constantly obtain the impossible has allowed me to live without berating myself for being stuck with a condition that I have no control over.

It costs a lot to look this cheap

The taste hierarchy is nothing more than a well-crafted lie maintained to help the same narrow group of people cling onto power with their cold, dead hands.

They use taste not to liberate us, or to make life enjoyable, but to assert their dominance over anyone not lucky enough to be born into bundles of cash.

I have always considered our sense of taste to be a primal instinct rather than an intellectual tool. Not taste in terms of the food we eat, but every other thing we inevitably choose to consume in our day-to-day lives. Most of the time, the reason we like the things we like seems predetermined by an unexplained force or part of our brain that is impossible to decode. It feels innate and emotional to be drawn to a particular object or piece of music, just as it feels unshiftable when we feel repulsed. Our sense of self is constantly evolving but ultimately immovable; we are drawn to the things that excite us for reasons that cannot be explained by logic or reason. But at some point, we learn to not fully trust our own taste. We accept that there are people who have better taste than us, and seek out those who can teach us how to fill our lives with the right kind of things.

It can be enjoyable to either challenge or conform to what is overarchingly accepted as good, or tasteful, or worthy of our headspace and money. It can be fun to lust over a specific bag or pair of shoes, just as we relish the opportunity to subvert popular trends in an attempt to create our own. But letting our taste be determined and judged by others – even when that means rejecting what is universally accepted as 'good' – also holds us back. The modern hierarchy of taste is not, as I once thought, a series of tools to be utilised in the quest for self-expression. Instead, it is a prescribed set of rules built on generations of class disparity. The people who invent the rules of taste are the same people who have gripped on to power for the whole of modern history. They use taste not to liberate us, or to make life enjoyable, but to assert their dominance over anyone not lucky enough to be born into bundles of cash. I came to learn that having 'good taste' is not dependent on how confident you are in yourself and your interests, but on how closely you can resemble the rich.

It wasn't until adulthood that I realised my family was poor. My revelation didn't come in one single moment, but rather a bombardment of seemingly minor events that finally helped me put together the pieces and conclude that the people around me lived completely different lives to mine. The countless times my peers have suggested I just ask my mum for money to fund private healthcare, as if this was a totally normal, cheap and reasonable request, probably contributed to my realisation. Or when I've arrived to parties dressed up to the nines for fear of someone calling me out for not looking rich enough, only to have someone in my group declare it a 'flex' to look like shit when walking through expensive venues.

It might have been after hearing for the umpteenth time how someone launched a fledgling business financed by their trust fund, or watching friends' Christmases on Instagram and discovering their sprawling country estates, their designer gifts and their swimming pools. Until I moved away from home, rich people were an abstract concept in my mind. They existed only on TV screens or in the pages of my hoarded magazines. I would pore over shoplifted high-fashion publications in awe of the clothes and speechless at the price tags, spend countless hours watching series after series about privileged teens and meticulously plot how to recreate my favourite high-fashion looks on a budget. I didn't spend much time feeling sorry for myself because my life wasn't the same as those of the people I admired – why would it be?

Who actually had a job or a rich enough family that saw them ferried around the major global city of their choice, buying whatever clothes they wanted and constantly attending events with open bars? It seemed impossibly glamorous to me, a teenager who spent her Friday nights drinking two-litre bottles of cider on the beach and shopping in Primark. It was always fairly obvious that my household didn't have as much disposable income as some of those I grew up with – I didn't go on the same holidays, dress in outfits from the same shops or have the same cultural references drilled into me from childhood. But my mum's lack of income didn't cause me to miss out on anything or prevent me from discovering the things I loved. OK, I wasn't buying Prada or drinking champagne stolen from my parents' drinks cabinet, but I found ways to get my hands on nearly everything I wanted, within reason.

I created workarounds for things I couldn't afford, and saved for things that were impossible to talk my way into. I was convinced that money was not the only way to get what I wanted, nor the only way to garner respect. I never had much, but I was always sure of who I was and what I liked. Above all, I was absolutely sure that I had good taste – despite the fact that I often didn't have the means to prove it. But when I moved to London, I inadvertently became one of the people I'd convinced myself were nothing more than fantasy – though without the connections, cash or confidence that ensured I would make it in the cut-throat world of fashion.

I didn't go to private school, had not a single family member who followed a remotely similar path to mine, and would have never even heard of a trust fund if it wasn't for *Gossip Girl* or *The Hills*. Though I grew up in a single-parent household, with a mum who relied on child tax credits and free school meals, by entering the magazine and publishing industry, I was always assumed to have come from money. As I stared at the people filling up the spaces I found myself in, I realised that they were nothing like the ones I grew up with. I was almost totally unaware that I was pining for acceptance in an industry that continues to only welcome the rich while being utterly obsessed with those who are poor.

My confusion at ending up in rooms full of birthright millionaires most likely came from a mistaken belief that taste was innate rather than learned. Growing up, I was encouraged to explore my sense of taste: to dye my hair garish colours that I would come to regret, to buy clothes that were the opposite of what everyone else around me was wearing, and to honestly be myself no matter the cost. I came to believe that taste was not a singular vision, but multiple splintering threads, and that even if you didn't fit in with the majority of people, you'd eventually find a place filled with those whose taste matched yours. I didn't believe in the moral superiority of liking the right things; I didn't really understand or have any knowledge of the class system, and I thought that actively pushing against the things that everybody else liked was the most exciting thing in the world.

But in London, instead of finding people who embraced the subjectivity and complexity of taste in the way I understood it, I realised that most people who gravitated towards the creative industries I aspired to be a part of did so as a way to uphold a code of taste that keeps people out, rather than welcoming them in. That the people who decide what we wear, watch, listen to and put in our homes are not there necessarily for love of those things, but because it is all they have ever known. Their 'good' taste isn't acquired through years of experiences that helped them develop a sense of who they are, but is rather passed down to them from family members who have always had access to the finer things in life.

In the original incarnation of *Gossip Girl*, Blair self-identifies as 'a dictator of taste'. She's judgemental, particular, and knows everything there is to know about clothes. Her mother is a fashion designer, she lives in a penthouse and is impossibly privileged. She is also a fictional character, and one I could have never imagined encountering in real life. I saw a lot of myself in Blair: her strong will, her bossiness, and her obsession with how what we wear is socially and politically important. Our similarities aside from fashion ideologies were non-existent; our upbringings couldn't have been further apart. What I failed to realise on my copious rewatches of the series was that Blair's title was fitting because of her background and not because of her passions. And that in my adult life, I would meet more 'dictators of taste' than I ever thought possible.

Class inequality is the unspoken infrastructure upon which so many industries claiming to be inclusive thrive, with those within elite spaces using their superior sense of taste to quash those they deem unworthy or who fall outside the margins of acceptability. But it can be hard to pinpoint the tangible ways in which the dominance of wealthy people affects our lives. So much of how the taste hierarchy intersects with classist elitism is murky and difficult to identify. When I try to tell my mum just how many heiresses, millionaires or children of nepotism I am surrounded by on a regular basis, it feels like I'm recounting some sort of far-fetched, fucked-up fairy tale. I can shock her with the facts, but what I fail to get across is just how much our lives are influenced by people who are desperate to cling to power by any means necessary.

As well as the fact that nearly all of our politicians and practically anyone else in a position of power went to private school, the statistic that the films we watch, our choice of clothes and the music we listen to is largely determined by the 1 per cent feels incomprehensible. Of the women who work in news media, 50 per cent of them attended one of the aforementioned educational institutions. 91 per cent of influencers are white, meaning only 9 per cent – regardless of class status – are people of colour. This creates a cultural landscape that is entirely unrepresentative of the people who actually populate the country, with the media being the modern dictators of taste who lord over our choices.

The choice of who we take seriously and who we ignore is deeply rooted in class disparity, with implications reaching far beyond someone's aesthetic choices or social media tattles. Our world views are crafted by those whose opportunities are fast-tracked due to wealth, and as a consequence, our perception of 'good' and 'bad' taste runs far deeper than the clothes we wear, and alters our perception of everything from feminism, well-being and disability, to beauty and gender. Because of the way in which society idolises the rich while berating the poor, we invalidate working-class people's experiences.

Taste can often seem frivolous, and it's easy to assume that no one really gets hurt when you look down on the fact that they love a pair of ugly shoes, have terrible taste in throw cushions, idolise shallow boy bands or earnestly love reality TV. But constantly criticising the things that other people enjoy has a wider effect on how we view whole groups of people, and how much we trust them with positions of power. By viewing their taste as inferior, we subconsciously render them less intellectually capable. We believe their perspectives are invalid and that they have no idea what's best for them; meaning we must be ruled by the rich and blindly follow how they tell us to live.

Taste, and its implication that some people are more worthy of power and respect than others, is used as a stick to beat working-class people. A woman at an expensive health retreat is chic, but a chronically ill person is a drain on our NHS. We see the former as somebody who puts her own needs first, and the latter as a dead weight to society. Rich women can recalibrate their whole lives to the pursuit of health, as long as they do so from the luxury of a mansion and allow us all to watch via our phone screens with voyeuristic glee, wishing we could whisk ourselves off to the Alps and eat a single cubed potato for breakfast, lunch and dinner.

Minimalism is an impossible aspiration when you're unwell and live most of your existence within the same four walls, but modern 'good taste' relishes scarcity. If you're seen to be taking up a lot of space, be it with the clothes you wear, your choice of decor, your political opinions or your need for medical help, you're trashy. Minimalism works on the assumption that you have all the choices in the world, yet reject those options in favour of a 'clean' life. I am unable to artfully curate my existence beyond which pills are to be taken at which time of day. There is no way of hiding the scattering of pill bottles, the heart rate monitors, and the piles of hospital letters that are pushed through my letter box on a daily basis. A clean, minimal life implies an affluent existence – and one that I will never achieve.

Much of the time, an obsession with 'bad taste' is only accepted when rich people indulge in the enjoyment of low aesthetics in a heavily dosed display of irony. A love of all things OTT has to be laced with a knowing sense that these things are not really being taken seriously. Traditional signifiers of wealth – jewels, gold, Versace-print everything, logo-adorned designer handbags and expensive cars – were co-opted by celebrity culture at some point in the early 2000s in a very American style of aspiration. All the things that told us somebody was rich became very, very trashy.

From Paris Hilton to the Kardashian family, being open about how much money you had started to be seen as cheap. As the aforementioned starlets became embroiled in sex-tape scandals and rose to public infamy when they chose to open up their lives to us common people through our TV screens, the wealthy had to find a new way to assert their dominance over the rest of us. Cold marble surfaces and the inclination to have literally nothing on display in any part of your home replaced a penchant for houses stuffed full of expensive artefacts. Pink, denim and diamanté clothing was eclipsed by plain beige silhouettes that signalled to the world that you could afford to spend £5,000 pounds on a coat that could have just as easily cost fifty.

These shifts in what we consider to be good taste also align with a move towards conservatism in the world. Wearing a Phoebe Philo era Celine suit may offer the illusion of an empowered woman, but in reality, we're mimicking stereotypical masculinity and reasserting that good taste is only viable when it upholds the cis-patriarchal status quo. But as the upper classes continue their obsession with minimalism, our sense of taste has become muddled, as we all become increasingly preoccupied with authenticity.

Authenticity is, rightly or wrongly, no longer considered possible when you're rolling in cash and people are becoming more acutely aware of the prevalence of nepotism and wealth when it comes to who we consider taste-makers. Whereas existing in the upper and middle classes used to be an immediate signifier that you knew all about the finer things in life, those who do come from money are going to greater and greater lengths to conceal their realities in order to prove they have earned their position of power rather than inherited it.

One scroll through social media and you're convinced the entire world is in the same position as you. The statistics, however, prove it's becoming more and more difficult to enter creative spaces without coming from a well-off family. Creative university courses in the UK are having their funding cut in half – meaning there will be even less support and visibility for low-income students looking to study anything outside of traditional subjects. The government is also removing the additional funding for arts universities in London, which helps subsidise the additional cost of education inside the capital city. These universities not only offer some of the best creative arts courses in the world, but also target students from low-income areas and support them in getting into higher education.

The student grant that saw me through my degree has already been scrapped, meaning my younger sister and millions of others like her will be lumped with increased debt and economic instability into adulthood. Even before I got to university, I received a weekly Educational Maintenance Allowance, which paid my bus fare to sixth-form college and meant I didn't miss out on materials needed for my studies. I was among the last cohort of students to benefit from the scheme, which was scrapped in 2011. For so many working-class people who operate in middle-class worlds, admitting that they have struggled growing up in poor households is something to be done with reluctance.

If you can hide the fact that you're different, it's often easier to do so, as no matter how much people want to tell you they aren't privileged, they often recoil when in the presence of someone who genuinely has experienced more poverty-stricken circumstances. My discomfort at being in spaces surrounded by the wealthy has only increased the longer I've operated within them. My once proud confidence in my own taste is chipped away at each time I am put in a room full of people in designer dresses with perfectly blow-dried hair. I'll forget every impressive thing I've ever done, and how good I felt I looked before I left the house. I'll feel unkempt no matter how put together I am, and inadequate no matter how much I know, deep down, that I deserve to be there.

In those moments, it feels impossible for good taste to transcend class when you're attempting to be taken seriously. But at the opposite end of the spectrum, there is a whole host of fairly wealthy people who are desperate to conceal that they are surrounded by money. People who are eager to convince those around them of their working-class credentials, despite the fact that their parents supplement their income and paid their deposit when they bought a property. As I found myself speaking to more and more people from middle- and upper-class backgrounds, I realised that they don't see being poor as a rigid socioeconomic standard dictated by your income and quality of life.

Instead, to many people, being 'poor' exists on an imaginary spectrum that genuinely hard-up people never have the pleasure to even consider. For some of them, it means not being able to afford dinner out multiple times a week, missing out on one of their four holidays abroad, or dipping into the savings accounts their parents set up for them. While growing up poor is actually debilitating in terms of opportunities and experiences, those who are rich have become ashamed to admit that their wealth may have helped them.

Instead, they decide to either keep quiet about their background or warp their origin story to align with working-class experiences. Influential people struggle to accept that they are rich, and spend their time fetishising the experiences of those who aren't. At the opposite end of the conversation, those who are poor or who grew up without abundance are left feeling gaslighted by the people they see wearing head-to-toe designer, living in their own flats and buying expensive furniture while in the same breath bragging about their latest claim to have no disposable cash left at the end of each month.

Watching the lives of America's young elite during my teenage years felt like fantastical, impossible escapism.

But discovering subculture – be it punk, riot grrrl or nu rave – felt tangible. These were people who lived scrappy lives, turned against the status quo and paved their own way to cultural and critical recognition. In my mind, they grew up in similar ways to me; and some of them actually did. But the majority of people I met who claimed to have come from nothing actually had a head start, whether in the form of wealth or connections, that eased the path to fulfilling their dreams.

These people speak in almost a secret language; they decide what's cool among themselves, are hostile to outsiders, and close ranks when anyone dares to question the system that awards them their positions as dictators of taste. Those without privilege who manage to push their ideas forward have to convince someone in an elite position that their work is worth the time of day. The illusion I grew up with, of believing that subculture's history was shaped by working-class kids, people of colour and those otherwise marginalised by society, quickly flew out the window.

The more people I met, the more I realised that the creative industries were run by people who could accept earning an income less than minimum wage because they lived their lives propped up by financial support from their parents. Not only that, but the assumption that it was possible to slip through the cracks and build a legacy without bundles of cash was little more than a well-crafted lie. The fashion industry, and the intersecting visual arts industries surrounding it, ran on a basis of trickle-up and trickle-down.

Until the fifties and sixties, trickle-down theory prevailed: working-class people were considered too culturally lacking to pioneer or create, and the upper classes dictated fashion trends and beauty norms, which then worked their way down into the mainstream. This is similar to how the high street operates now: we see the Miu Miu runway, and six months later, similar items start popping up in H&M. However, beginning halfway through the twentieth century, and continuing right up to the present day, trickle-up theory is thought to be more culturally relevant in contemporary arts and culture. It refers to trends originating in working-class or marginalised cultures that then penetrate class barriers and are adopted by those in the upper echelons of society. Denim becoming socially acceptable in the sixties, the grunge movement of the nineties, and even T-shirts transforming from military wear to everyday essentials are all examples of this.

Trickle-up theory can be observed in practically every cultural movement and trend we see today, whether it's a fickle obsession with diversity, streetwear, or the thousands of micro-trends we see across our Instagram Explore pages on a regular basis. For a long time, I considered trickle-up to be a win for progression. I understood it as a way for marginalised people to have their contributions recognised. But the longer I spent observing these trends, the more I understood trickle-up culture as another way to exploit people who innovate but do not have the resources to capitalise on their own ideas.

No matter how genuinely interesting or original a piece of clothing, music, art or writing is, your success is capped – both monetarily and in terms of reach – unless someone further up the social food chain can profit from it. Part of the reason why this problem still prevails is that we are obsessed with acceptance; people who have been left on the outside naturally crave to be let in, and it's difficult to trust in the power of our own ideas when they have been diminished for so long.

Separately, trickle-up theory has been mutating since the advent of the internet. Now, it's easier than ever to access alternative ideas – and it's also far easier to get away with packaging yourself as subversive when you aren't, as social media seemingly flattens social divides and places us all on the same platform. Where we apply trickle-up theory, we are more often than not actually referring to a fetishisation of youth culture, regardless of social class. We look to teenagers and young adults to dictate trends and taste on a micro-level online, taking them at face value. Influencers and cultural pioneers are often guilty of presenting as poor online, in a bid to be relatable to their audiences, when in actuality their lives more closely resemble royalty than roughing it.

*

My adulthood has been an intricately spun spider web of navigating situations in which taste has provided a smoke-screen for class. As I struggled with the idea of acceptance by people I would never be able to relate to in the fashion industry, equally, when trying to enter DIY spaces, I was already considered a sell-out. I've always straddled a space between DIY publishing and the moneyed magazine industry; my publication has the polished veneer of something that requires cash to produce, but everything I've ever made has been put together for practically zero budget. There is no secret investor, bank of mum and dad or even consistent source of income.

What I realised is that being authentic in DIY spaces is practically the same as being considered legitimate in upper-class environments; both require a prescriptive set of rules regarding taste. In both cases, these requirements are predetermined and dictated to you rather than mutually agreed upon. For both worlds, my taste was too garish, too pink, I liked girlie things too much and hadn't read the right books. Although the DIY community prides itself on doing a lot for very little and rejecting binaries of taste, it too operates on its own standards. If your zine isn't cut-and-pasted or photocopied black and white, and if your shirt isn't thrifted or your shoes dirty, you're a fraud. I was considered inauthentic in these spaces as much as I felt unwelcome in spaces in which women exclusively carried Chanel handbags.

But being content in having very little is a privilege in and of itself – if you have the time and resources to keep creating without any pressure of making money from it at some point, you're likely to have a level of security that many never experience. Taste tyranny does not only exist in the upper echelons of society. In the same way that creative authenticity has come to be represented by a punk aesthetic that was innovated over fifty years ago, rich women will scoff at you for having never tried a particular food or mispronouncing a fashion designer's name. The purpose of taste in this context is to both retain control and assert power. Whereas I believe taste can help us find common ground, in more instances than not it is actually used to divide us.

One weekend, I was tabling at zine fairs, and the following day I was attending events and taking meetings in private members' clubs where the price of lunch ate up my entire weekly income. Neither situation made me feel welcome. Even though I had my foot in the door, my growth felt stunted. I couldn't keep up with a constantly rotating wardrobe of new designer clothes, expensive after-work drinks and unpaid commissions. I had to face the fact that my family's income set me apart from most of the other people around me, and that no matter how good my taste was, it would never be accepted by people determined to uphold their own positions of power. More accurately, I had anti-imposter syndrome. I didn't believe

I was undeserving of my place in the internships or jobs I found myself in, but I very quickly realised that there was absolutely nobody else remotely like me occupying the desks I sat at.

I approached everything I did with a bullish confidence, largely unfazed, not yet understanding that these worlds operated largely on nepotism and gatekeeping in order to maintain an archaic social order. I genuinely believed that working hard enough and wanting it enough would see me soar to the highest heights and had no qualms about putting myself in front of extremely intimidating people and in anxiety-inducing situations in order to get what I wanted. While many feel that they have not fully earned the merits that have landed them in the professional spaces they occupy, I and other marginalised people are genuinely treated with hostility.

Imposter syndrome operates on the assumption that our feelings of inadequacy are all in our head, and that it's our own self-deprecation holding us back as we allow our anxieties to dictate how we feel about our career pro-gression. For marginalised people, this is a lie. Yes, we are prone to feeling we aren't good enough, or to questioning our taste, just as everybody else is. But unlike middle- and upper-class people, we have actual evidence to back up our fears. Not only is there likely to be no one – or very few people – with experiences that echo ours in the room, but the isolation that arises from existing in spaces that you cannot relate to on any level convinces you that it's impossible to thrive at all.

Part of the reason I started my zine, *Polyester*, was that as I began studying fashion, arts and culture, I quickly became disenchanted with how entire industries were built on intellectual elitism and liking the right things. I was bored of being told that happiness came in the form of a white marble coffee table, that wearing all-black avant-garde clothing made by a small group of designers meant you instantly exuded an aura of intellectualism, and that there were right and wrong ways to care about culture. I didn't understand why my way into learning about the things I cared about – or the things I cared about themselves – was dismissed as unimportant. During university, I went through a phase of exclusively shopping at COS and trying to palm it off as Comme des Garçons, but my foray into only wearing sharp cuts and pretending I didn't live for leopard print was short-lived.

Trying to cosplay as someone who had money always had me feeling as though I was running to catch up with those around me; it was exhausting, unfulfilling and futile. At a time in my life at which I felt most vulnerable – sick, surrounded by people I couldn't relate to and living away from my family – I decided to embrace what I had always loved, rather than constantly trying to climb upwards and away from my true interests and beliefs. I've never enjoyed the idea of having less stuff. By unashamedly embracing the things I had previously felt embarrassed at finding joy in, I live a happier life. My floor is covered in a sprawling zebra-print rug, next to a plush pink velvet headboard that frames multiple prints and works of art that bring me peace when I feel most cut off from the world. Through my zine, I found other people who felt the same way as me and had grown up under similar circumstances. I learned that my interest in the bright, the garish, the girlie and the gruesome wasn't devoid of merit, thought or feeling.

Using the pope of trash himself, John Waters, as my guide, I became confident in my belief that trying to appeal to everyone – or even those in closest proximity to you – isn't as important as finding people who truly understand why seemingly meaningless objects, aesthetics, films, bands or clothes can help build the emotional basis of who you are. Most importantly, I began to understand that our concept of what is good and what is bad was created by people I have absolutely no interest in trying to impress.

The internet allowed me to find this community, and to understand that my 'guilty' pleasures were not guilty at all. My peers, many of whom transcended the URL world and became IRL friendships, taught me that feeling ashamed of what we enjoy is likely because of a centuries-old class system that seeks to keep marginalised people in their place at the bottom and gatekeep what constitutes important culture. But discovering all these things and people not only helped me feel less alone, it also helped me build the beginnings of a business.

Younger millennials and Gen Z have spent a large part of their formative years and early adulthood being sold a lie that the invention of the internet and subsequent social media boom would cause the democratisation of these jealously guarded industries. It's something I also truly believed, after watching people I knew online grow from shooting themselves in their homes to lensing covers of *Vogue*. However, the golden age of accumulating thousands of followers in order to kick-start your career is long gone. The lines of social hierarchy, once rigid and painfully obvious, are now blurred, murky and almost impossible to decipher. Where the lie of meritocracy has traditionally warped our world view, the invention of social media added a whole new host of class-related complications to the mix.

We assume that those with thousands, hundreds of thousands or even millions of followers are making bank from their online presence. We genuinely believe that online popularity crosses over into actual tangible economic success. However, this is not the case. Those who can successfully convert their online influence into a career likely already have access to the life they crave in the first place. My publication was born out of survival; a way to penetrate a notoriously difficult industry and earn a living while creating space for what I loved. For others, their activist collectives or feminist Instagram accounts were important projects, but came with no pressure to pay the bills.

But as the taste/class divide blurs, we have an opportunity to completely pull apart the systems that have held those with 'bad' taste back. The advancement of technology and social media has allowed each and every one of us to transcend our means and build the platforms we have always dreamed of with very little money. While I have never stretched *Polyester* beyond its limit – aka the amount of money in the business account – I have been able to put together full printed publications on a shoestring and earn enough money to self-fund the publication for nearly a decade. While capitalism may feel inescapable, we're now freer than ever to indulge in the taste we truly love.

We can choose who we invest in through likes, followers and screen time. It's never been easier to reject the taste binary and find people who adore the same horribly gaudy things as you do. There is a future in which we can take our power back from those who refuse to let us in. We no longer need to rely on archaic industries for validation, or exposure, or even our income. Using the internet, and harnessing the power in difference, we can create new systems built on inclusivity rather than impossible aspiration. Currently, we expect internet fame to lead us on a path of traditional success.

But as long as traditional success is steeped in racism, sexism, ableism, fatphobia and classism, none of us should be wishing it upon ourselves. We have to shed the belief that the only way to be successful is to echo the systems of power that have ensured we will never match the success of those who are born into it. The taste hierarchy is nothing more than a well-crafted lie, maintained to help the same narrow group of people cling on to power with their cold dead hands. By smashing it to pieces, a brighter world full of gloriously garish taste is possible.

Epilogue –
have faith in your
own bad taste

Authenticity is ultimately a trap, just as the fear of being too much is. They work together to make us feel as if we will never be good enough, and that we will never know enough. Aspiring to either one makes change absolutely impossible.

I have always feared being 'too much'. I'm terrified of talking too much after too many drinks, of being too bossy, of being overdressed for the occasion, of asking too much of other people and being too needy. Dealing with myself is like persistently arguing with the most high-maintenance person in the world; I'm constantly fighting an internal battle of wanting to do the most while being absolutely terrified of opening myself up to the vulnerability that comes with holding nothing back.

Illness in many ways forced me to accept that being perceived as vulnerable is largely out of my control. There is literally no way to be chronically sick without letting others see that you aren't absolutely stoic all of the time. Becoming unwell helped me realise that the only person I was harming through fear of being too much was myself. That really, nobody else cares if I post too many selfies on Instagram or if my dress is too extravagant for happy hour. But every so often, the dread that comes with facing myself for who I truly am creeps in.

I question every decision I've ever made, every belief I hold, every outfit I own and every sentence I've ever spoken. I text ten of my friends to ask if I'm annoying, or cringe while frantically watching and deleting my own

Instagram stories. I don't think I'm alone in this. Nor do I think the fear of being too much only affects our individual minds and well-being. The fact that we all think we're too much isn't just an irrational collective anxiety, but a deliberate gendered tactic to stunt not only personal development but also societal progression. The fact that so much of marginalised people's behaviour is already policed forces us to be the smallest versions of ourselves in order to create minimal friction as we move through the world. But as we took up feminism, it felt as though enough was enough. We were collectively rejecting the notion that our identities inherently meant we had to constantly self-censor to be taken seriously.

On the surface, tackling these issues is a way to break down the societal factors that cause us to feel like we're too much. For a while, the rise of sociopolitical discourse both online and in physical spaces felt like slowly breaking these boundaries down one by one: we started to teach each other that everything we knew about gender, or being fat, or poor, or chronically ill, was decided by a system that had no intention of caring for us. But then the fear of being too much slowly began to reinfect all of our minds. We began to second-guess our ability to change the world, so settled with self-optimising instead.

I believe the backwards way we are now approaching sociopolitical issues, be it feminism, self-care, fatphobia, ableism, classism or anything else, can be traced back to a fear of being too much. Somewhere between constantly being censored by social media algorithms, having our politics dictated to us, the commodification of fourth-wave feminism and the glorification of girl bosses, we began to doubt our own ability to build successful sociopolitical movements. Instead of using this new power to shatter the systems that harm us, we have come to accept that liberating oneself is as good as it gets when it comes to fighting for equal rights. We believe that feminism is either shallow, individualist and only suitable for feminine hygiene adverts, or it's governmental, ruled by policy and work done by 'real' activists as opposed to anyone with an Instagram account. The former leaves many of us feeling above it all, with the latter alienating huge swathes of us who don't see ourselves as educated enough to participate.

We're stuck in a stalemate in which we feel the most informed we ever have, at the exact moment we feel totally powerless. I've never considered feminism to be one thing alone; it's not just the fight for equal pay, or parental rights, or only for cisgender women and only legitimate when pushed through our democratic system. But our fear of too much results in an obsession with categorising and then splintering every single adjacent sociopolitical issue. If we can't be an expert in everything, then our fear of being called out for assuming too much can be quashed by homing in on a single facet of identity politics. Fat liberation is seen as a separate issue to gender politics, which exists apart from racial justice, gay rights and disability activism. No one can be totally informed in every single strand of activism, but failing to embrace the similarities and differences in our experiences continues to ensure that nothing we care about progresses upwards.

Over a decade into the rise of social media, many of us find ourselves existing within a paradox. We're terrified of the consequences of being ourselves while also expecting absolute authenticity from everyone around us. This doesn't just apply to social politics; so many of our personal brands are tied up in not just the clothes we wear, or who we hang out with, but in what we believe in too. Because of this, we've reached a stalemate in the representation of our lives and the issues we care about, particularly in the online realm.

We crave the attention we glean from posting online just as we wish for the change that could come from standing up for what we believe in, but are terrified of being exposed and criticised for earnestly presenting ourselves. As a result, we are witnessing the best of neither world. We are watching the issues we care about being absolutely bastardised by people who have never had to worry about being too much and who can twist social politics to appease their own desires. We can all see that individualist empowerment has absolutely minimal benefit to the majority of us, but fail to see an effective route to collective empowerment without leaving ourselves vulnerable to the thing we fear the most: being exposed as ill-informed and inauthentic.

We've somehow come to the conclusion that being wrong is the worst thing you can be. But it's better to be proven wrong about something you initially hated than coming to the realisation that you placed your hope into the wrong hands. The reason we're drawn to spending our time fighting it out in the comments section is because cynicism is a far easier road to follow than true vulnerability. It's far more painless to deploy snark than openly admitting to loving something in all its earnestness. Our discourse surrounding social politics seems so catty because we spend all of our energy trying to convince other people that they are the ones who are too much, and that they've got it all wrong, rather than seeking out solutions that will result in collective joy.

Criticism is not all snark and judgement; it has the power to positively impact not just individuals, but the direction of social movements too. So much of my adult life has been spent trying to convert cynicism into positive alternatives. Instead of falling down the rabbit hole of criticism for the sake of criticism, I turned to creating the things I wanted to see and spaces that I believed needed to exist. Now, we feel powerless that the possibility of creating a better world seems so totally out of our hands, and that blind criticism is the only form of power or control we have left.

We need to shatter the belief that authenticity is the

only way out of the mess we have found ourselves in. Authenticity, when deployed online, is an impossible plight. We've built the foundations of our online selves on the basis that what we show to the world is a curation and not the whole picture. That the internet is a chance to show off how funny, or how clever, or how beautiful we are – while equally expecting it to provide us a space in which to grow, and learn, and become better people. Online spaces provide the illusion that we are all experts when discussing information or issues on our own profiles.

We believe that the only effective way of speaking on an issue is to learn absolutely everything there is to know and spread the gospel accordingly. We view the people we follow as authority figures instead of peers. This fuels our fear of being too much, placing other people on a pedestal that is impossible to match or climb to, ultimately leaving many of us feeling as though we cannot use our voices. Authenticity is ultimately a trap, just as the fear of being too much is. They work together to make us feel we will never be good enough, and that we will never know enough. Aspiring to either one makes change absolutely impossible.

We need to shift away from authenticity and towards earnestness; to embracing our own too-muchness, to celebrating messiness, and to start approaching the online world in the same way we do our real lives. Our existences are only set to become more digitised, and presenting ourselves as prim and proper serves no real purpose other than self-sanitising who we truly are. Just as we all go out, chat shit, and spend the next forty-eight hours replaying every single thing we said back in our minds in case we showed ourselves up, we need to accept that discourse online will not always or immediately be gratifying. That building a better world means saying stupid things and learning from them. That admitting to the things we love is not embarrassing, but liberating. That there is literally no such thing as being too much. And that having faith in our own bad taste is the only chance we have of getting out of this mess.

References

Chris Kraus, *I Love Dick* (1997)

Llewellyn Louderback, 'More People Should Be FAT' (1967)

Grace Nichols, *The Fat Black Woman's Poems* (1984)

Edgar Allen Poe, *The Philosophy of Composition* (1846)

Acknowledgements

First of all, thank you to my mum. Thank you for making me believe in myself, and forcing me to always be myself no matter the cost. There is no one more creative or more brilliant than you. To my family – Pammygram, Daisy, Amanda, Koren and Nina: all I can say is thank God I was raised almost entirely by a group of women; thank you for making me who I am. Thank you to Sharmaine for believing in this book before I even considered it to be a collection of work that could exist. And thank you to Kate, my agent, for opening my unsolicited DM one week into the first lockdown while we were all going insane, and signing me. You've helped shape this book into what I always hoped it would be. I couldn't have done it without you or our many, many conversations where you patiently helped me unpick my complaints about the world. Thank you to the whole of Dialogue Books, to Millie and Amy and Celeste and Emily and everyone else. And to Maisie for editing *Poor Little Sick Girls* with such thoughtfulness.

I don't think I would have been able to write even a sentence of this book without spending nearly a decade in the best community and group of friends I could ever hope for. Thank you, Gina Tonic, for always ranting, crying, laughing and eating snacks with me. I'll always be grateful to you for being by my side through literally everything and for basically being the best chosen sister I could ever hope for. I wouldn't have trusted anyone else to run *Polyester* with me while I wrote this book. Thank you to the entire *Polyester* team: Halima, Gina S, Hatti, Eden, Charlotte, Grace, Clarissa and Olivia. You've taught me that work doesn't actually have to be completely grim, you always push me to make *Polyester* the best it can be, and help me shape the type of world we should all be able to exist in.

Thank you to Polly, not only for creating the most gorgeous cover in the entire world but for spending countless evenings drinking wine with me, resulting in so many of the conversations that would end up in this book. Edward, thanks for dealing with me as a big-headed twenty-year-old and sticking with me through all these years. You've helped me shape my world view more than you know – love you for ever for listening to every single thought that enters my brain and for helping me make sense of them.

The Whole Shiraz quite literally kept me from losing my mind during the pandemic: Bridget, Amber, Misha, Jen, Rachel, I love you. Thank you for being my chosen rats in this life. You've all pulled me out from the rubble of despair when it came to the hard points in this book, and I love nothing more than chatting absolute shit with every single one of you. Rakel, Rene and Maggie, you make London what it is for me. You've taught me so much not only about friendship but also about chosen family. Camille, thank you for being the person I have the best times with, who I can talk to for days without getting bored, and for probably being the only one I could do an eight-hour road trip with. Maria, thanks for getting me started on all of this. My teens would have been nothing without you. I feel so grateful we got to learn and be messy beside each other. Thank you to Kenzie, Rosa and Honey for teaching me the power of sick sad girl friendship.

Sirin, thank you for commissioning the essay that started all of this. Your belief in me proves how warm your heart is despite the fact that you insist you have no emotions. And Hannah, Daisy, Dominique, Lauren, Kieran, I feel so lucky to consider you all my peers. You literally have the best minds, and I can't believe I get to call you my friends.

Alfie, there are no words that would properly encapsulate all the things I have to thank you for. I wouldn't want to do any of this without you.

Bringing a book from manuscript to what you are reading is a team effort.

Dialogue Books would like to thank everyone who helped to publish *Poor Little Sick Girls* in the UK.

Editorial
Sharmaine Lovegrove
Amy Baxter
Joanna Kramer

Contracts
Stephanie Cockburn

Sales
Caitriona Row
Dominic Smith
Frances Doyle
Hannah Methuen
Lucy Hine
Toluwalope Ayo-Ajala

Design
Charlotte Stroomer
Polly Nor
Jo Taylor

Production
Narges Nojoumi
Zahraa Al-Hussaini

Publicity
Millie Seaward

Marketing
Emily Moran

Copy-Editor
Jane Selley

Proofreader
David Bamford

Operations
Kellie Barnfield
Millie Gibson
Sanjeev Braich